How to
Be a Hero

Train with the Saints

by Julia Harrell

with illustrations by
Chad Thompson

Pauline
BOOKS & MEDIA
Boston

Library of Congress Control Number: 2016958842

CIP data is on file.
ISBN 10: 0-8198-3453-X
ISBN 13: 978-0-8198-3453-9

The Scripture quotations contained herein are from the *New Revised Standard Version Bible: Catholic Edition*, copyright © 1989, 1993, Division of Christian Education of the National Council of the Churches of Christ in the United States of America. Used by permission. All rights reserved.

Excerpts from the English translation of the *Catechism of the Catholic Church* for use in the United States of America, copyright © 1994, United States Catholic Conference, Inc.—Libreria Editrice Vaticana. Used with permission.

Design by Mary Joseph Peterson, FSP

With illustrations by Chad Thompson

Published by Pauline Books & Media, 50 Saint Pauls Avenue, Boston, MA 02130–3491

Printed in the U.S.A.

HTBH VSAUSAPEOILL12-1210080 3453-X

www.pauline.org

Pauline Books & Media is the publishing house of the Daughters of St. Paul, an international congregation of women religious serving the Church with the communications media.

1 2 3 4 5 6 7 8 9   21 20 19 18 17

For Will and Bridget

Contents

Introduction

If you could have any superpower, what would it be? Maybe you wish you could fly. Or maybe you would like to be able to read minds, or see through walls, or scale the side of a sky-scraper. Whatever superpower you chose would not only enable you to do amazing things, it would also set you apart from ordinary people. It would make you extraordinary in some way.

You may never have thought of it this way, but the people we honor as saints have something like superpowers. Instead of extraordinary strength or x-ray vision, though, the superpowers of the saints are the virtues. Part of what it takes for the Church to declare someone a saint is the practice of virtue in a big—or heroic—way. This means that a person has shown extraordinary virtue when interacting with other people and in serving God.

All Christians are called to grow in virtue. But what is virtue? The word virtue comes from a Latin word that means strength, courage, and power. A person who possesses a virtue is in the habit of doing the right thing for the right reasons. In other words, virtue makes someone a good person who does good things. People who are virtuous want to be good and show their goodness in their actions. Christian virtues are superpowers because they come from God's goodness and give us the strength to do amazing things for him.

Saints don't become virtuous all on their own but by God's grace and the Holy Spirit. Strengthened by prayer and the sacraments, they are filled with God's superpowers. Their journey of faith begins with Baptism, just as it does for every one of us. Like superheroes and star athletes, it's dedication to training and practice that makes them outstanding.

A virtuous Christian wants to be like Jesus—the greatest hero ever. There isn't just one way to be virtuous, though. The saints show us that there are many different ways to practice all of the virtues. And the way one virtue looks in one saint's life can be quite different from how it looks in another saint's life. While the saints each live the virtues in a unique way, they are united by the grace that comes from God to enable them to become more like Jesus.

This book is a training manual.

In it, we'll learn about the different kinds and categories of virtue so that we can hone our gifts and become heroes of virtue ourselves. That's why we'll meet saints who fought back against the Nazis, forgave their kidnappers, and left behind a life of addiction in order to follow God. They are some of the very best virtue coaches we can find. And, they're more than willing to train with us! In the process, we'll discover that virtue is possible for everyone: priests and religious brothers and sisters, mothers and fathers, the elderly and children—even you!

Part I

The Cardinal Virtues

Can you think of a time you set a goal for yourself—maybe you were trying out for a sports team or taking an important test? You probably have goals for the future too. Let's say your goal is to be the best swimmer in your school. If you want to be great, you have to train your body and mind.

You start with nutrition. If you put junk food into your body, you know it won't be able to perform as well. So you are careful to eat healthy, nutritious foods that will give you energy and help you grow. You know that there are many experienced and knowledgeable athletes out there with good advice for you, so you spend time talking and listening to them, absorbing their wisdom. You study the rules and theory of your sport. You read books and articles and spend time watching videos of the sport.

But, most importantly, you get out there and practice—not just when you feel like it or when it's convenient —every single day. You lift weights and run and stretch and do swimming drills. You practice the same thing over and over again until you get it right *every time*. That is how you become an excellent swimmer.

Even the very best need inspiration, coaching, equipment, and skills. Likewise, saints don't become virtuous and holy all by themselves. They do it with the guidance of the Holy Spirit, the grace of the sacraments, the inspiration of the saints who came before them, the Bible, prayer, and by trying again even when they fail.

When we do what we can to learn about God, seek out the sacraments, pray, and practice doing good, we grow in the four *cardinal virtues*: prudence, justice, fortitude, and temperance. The word "cardinal" comes from the Latin word *cardo*, which means "hinge." These four virtues are the hinges of the door that opens our hearts to even more virtues. Through our human effort cooperating with God's grace, we can develop the cardinal virtues and become holy like the saints.

That's also the kind of dedication it takes to become a saint. If we want to learn about God, to know who he is and how he wants us to live, we need to be fully open to God's grace working in our lives. But we have to do our part too. In other words, we train to be saints, and not just when we feel like it or when it's convenient.

Of course, athletes don't become champions all alone.

Chapter 1

Prudence and Pope Saint John Paul II

What Is Prudence?

Prudence helps us to know what is really good and to make the right choice in any situation. Prudence is a way of looking at things with "open eyes." Jesus taught his disciples about prudence when he told the parable of a king going to war. He asked his listeners if this king would "not sit down first and consider whether he is able with ten thousand to oppose the one who comes against him with twenty thousand? If he cannot, then, while the other is still far away, he sends a delegation and asks for the terms of peace" (Luke 14:31–32). The prudent king makes a wise choice about the best way to achieve his goal, rather than rushing in without thinking.

> I, wisdom,
>   live with prudence,
> and I attain knowledge
>   and discretion. . . .
> I have good advice and sound
>   wisdom;
> I have insight, I have
>   strength.
>
> Proverbs 8:12, 14

Prudence is using God's gifts of intellect and reason to make choices according to our faith. Our faith tells us what is true, and reason helps us understand why it is true. Prudence helps us use our reason to make the right choice about how to achieve a good goal. When a thinking mind and a believing heart work together, we are at our best!

People who climb Mount Everest hire professional local guides to accompany them on the journey. Climbers must be guided by a professional if they want to reach the top of the mountain and return safely to base camp. A knowledgeable guide has the experience and informed judgment to determine when a person needs medical care and when they are just tired,

when it is safe to continue climbing or when the weather is too bad or an avalanche is likely. Climbers need a guide to keep them safe, but also to push them on when they are fatigued and discouraged in order to reach their goal—the summit.

Prudence acts as a guide in the journey of life. Prudence helps us to know whether it is time to act or time to wait. Prudence warns you to run away from danger when you are not strong enough to battle against it successfully. But it also shows you when to stay and fight for truth and goodness. Prudence guides the other virtues by helping them work together and keeping them from going off-track. It is called the "chariot driver of the virtues" because it steers the conscience to practice virtue in all areas of our life.

Who Is Pope Saint John Paul II?

Poland, during the 1940s

The small group of friends moved swiftly through the pitch-black streets of Krakow, Poland. Snatches of whispered conversation passed between them as they sneaked through empty, dark neighborhoods, avoiding the roaming Nazi patrols.

After what seemed like an eternity, the friends reached their destination, an apartment in Krakow's Debniki neighborhood. Silently, they climbed the stairs and closed the door behind them. Though they were relieved to have made it safely inside, only dim lights were lit and a cautious atmosphere remained. More people began to arrive in a slow trickle, just one or two at a time. The people closed the blinds and, once everyone had arrived, they pushed the furniture back against the walls and prepared for a secret performance by a group of actors called the Rhapsodic Theatre.

Before the performance began, a twenty-one-year-old actor named Karol Wojtyla warned, "It is essential to keep these get-togethers secret; otherwise we risk serious punishment from the Nazis, even deportation to the concentration camps." No one doubted the graveness of the

situation or the truth of Karol's words, but neither did they make a move to leave. Bound together by their secret and their resolve to resist the Nazis, the young people remained huddled in this little apartment, as though they were gathering around a warm, bright fire in the midst of a dark and frigid wilderness.

Because the Rhapsodic Theatre was a secret group with very little money, Karol had no costume or props. Only his authoritative presence and clear, ringing voice commanded the attention of his audience.

"Oh, my homeland!" Karol began to recite lines from a poem that told the story of how Polish villagers revolted against occupying Russian troops.

As he spoke, the sound of a Nazi tank rolling along the street below could be heard outside the window. The tank moved slowly by; Nazi slogans and propaganda boomed from a crackling megaphone into the dark night. In the apartment three stories above the street, however, the cacophony fell on deaf ears. Karol never faltered in the delivery of his lines.

The script from which he recited portrayed a man grieving the loss of his beloved country at the hands of foreign army troops. It expressed what every Polish citizen felt. Like the characters in the play, they, too, were experiencing normal everyday things while living in a very abnormal environment, under the control of a foreign military. Again, like the play's villagers, they were fighting the invaders of their day, not with guns and swords, but with words and ideas. The Nazis had closed Poland's libraries, museums, and theaters. Polish citizens could be shot for going to the theatre, or even for speaking the Polish language within earshot of the wrong person.

Karol knew he could not simply remain silent, waiting passively for the occupation to come to an end as his country and heritage were being destroyed. He grieved the loss of art, theatre, and books in his homeland. Longingly, Karol remembered a time in which the Polish people had more to look forward to than waiting in line for food rations. He wanted to help people remember the cultural heritage that made them who they were.

Karol fought back by making a space for beauty and truth in a world filled with ugliness and lies. Karol took part in twenty-two formal performances and over one hundred rehearsals. As a teen, he had dreamed of becoming an actor, and it seemed as though the Rhapsodic Theatre would be the beginning of his promising acting career. Eventually though, Karol concluded that the theatre was not the lifelong vocation to which God was calling him.

Nonetheless, the wartime theatre group had prepared him to answer his true calling to become a priest. Because Polish Catholics were among the groups targeted by the Nazis, young Catholic men could not study openly for the priesthood. Karol and several other men attended secret classes at the archbishop's home.

Karol had learned how to resist the Nazis in a hidden way when he was a member of the Rhapsodic Theatre. In order to keep his seminary studies and preparation for the priesthood a secret, Karol continued to work at his full-time job at a stone quarry so he would not arouse suspi-

cion about what he was doing with his time. After the war ended a few years later, he was ordained Father Wojtyla, a parish priest. Eventually he became the archbishop of the large city of Krakow during the difficult period of Communist rule. Finally, Karol Wojtyla was elected to the role for which he is best known—pope. Afterward he took the name John Paul II.

Pope Saint John Paul II was a man of true prudence. Even as a young man, he understood that the occupying Nazi forces were destroying Poland, her people, and her cultural treasures. He realized that the ideas the Nazi party stood for were dangerous and evil, and that millions of innocent men, women, and children were losing their lives in Nazi concentration camps. The man who would become Pope John Paul II believed that, as a Catholic Christian and as a man of goodwill, he was compelled to resist the Nazis in some way. He was smart enough, however, to know that standing on the street corner with his own megaphone, shouting back at the Nazi troops as they rolled through the city, would not bring peace or end the Nazi occupation.

The Rhapsodic Theatre is where young Karol first practiced the art of proclaiming powerful truths in the face of dangerous lies. Though his stage and his audience would eventually far outstrip those very first ones in a small, dark apartment, this art would serve him well as he became a parish priest, and a bishop, and, finally, the pope. As a young man, Karol Wojtyla reflected on his own personal talents and how they could be used to fight the Nazis secretly. As a gifted actor and speaker, he was well-educated and familiar with Polish literature and art. He believed that words had power and the ability to communicate beauty and truth. Prudently, he chose resistance through words.

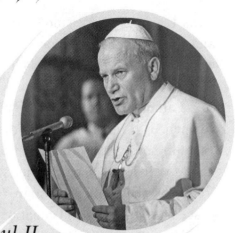

*Pope Saint John Paul II
was prudent because
he used his individual gifts
and skills to resist
the evils of Nazism in a wise
and inspirational way.*

● ●
Prayer for Prudence

Dear God of Wisdom,
please give me the grace to listen to the voice
of your Holy Spirit and the voices of wise
people in my life when I have a decision to
make. Help me see the truth in the situations
and choices I face everyday. Give me the light
to see what is truly right and good and the
strength to follow where you call me. Amen.

How Can I Train to Be a Hero of Prudence?

Is it easier to make prudent choices when I am calm, or when I am angry, frustrated, or afraid? Why? What can I do to calm myself in a difficult situation?

When I am looking for an example to follow or wondering about what direction to take, who are some people I can look to?

What can I do to prudently consider all my choices and their consequences before making a decision?

Honesty with myself is an important part of prudence. How can I know if I am being honest with myself? What might I do to be sure?

When I have a choice to make, how can my faith help me decide what to do?

Chapter 2

Justice and Blessed Pier Giorgio Frassati

What Is Justice?

Justice is giving to others what is owed to them. When we are just in our relationship with God, we give what is due to him. We worship God, adore him, and thank him for the many gifts he has given to us. We also practice justice in our relationships with our neighbors. We repay our debts; we are honest; we treat others with respect and care.

Jesus entered the Temple of Jerusalem and was furious about all of the abuses taking place.

[He] drove out all who were selling and buying in the Temple, and he overturned the tables of the money changers and the seats of those who sold doves. He said to them, "It is written,

> . . . cease to do evil,
> learn to do good;
> seek justice,
> rescue the oppressed,
> defend the orphan,
> plead for the widow.
>
> Isaiah 1:16b–17

'My house shall be called a house of prayer, but you are making it a den of robbers.' "

(Matthew 21:12–13)

For Jews, the Temple of Jerusalem was the heart of worship and prayer. Yet, some were exploiting those who came to worship there by charging unfair exchange rates and selling sacrificial animals for a steep price. Jesus wanted to restore justice by protecting this space for worship and promoting fair treatment of all those who came to the Temple to pray.

When we talk about the "justice system," we are usually referring to the way criminals are punished for their actions. This is part of justice, too. If we do something to hurt someone else, we are responsible for doing what we can to make amends and right the wrongs we have caused. For instance, in the case of theft, justice demands that the stolen money is repaid or the stolen item replaced. Sometimes, it is not possible to "fix" a wrong. We may not be able to restore or replace something that has been destroyed; or if we have injured someone, it may not be possible for them to get better.

Justice also includes accepting the consequences, good and bad, for our choices and actions. If you work, it is *just* that you get paid. If you tell a lie, it is *just* that you lose the trust of the person you lied to.

But justice is more than simply making up for our wrongs. Justice is also acknowledging what we have received, and using those gifts to make changes that address the problems in our world. Jesus said that whatever we do for others, we are also doing for him. When we use what we have to help someone else, it is a way of "repaying" God for all we have been given.

Who Is Blessed Pier Giorgio Frassati?

Italy, during the 1920s

Knock, knock, knock. Again the faint rapping sound came from the front door of the Frassati family's home.

"I think *you* should go see who is there, Pier Giorgio," advised his sister, Luciana.

The children opened the door. A mother and her little boy were standing outside in the freezing cold. Their clothes were old and tattered, and both mother and child were thin and shivering in the harsh winter wind. The boy hid his face in his mother's side, his arms wrapped tightly around his body as he tried to stay warm.

"I am sorry to disturb you at this late hour," began the woman, "but we haven't had anything to eat for two days.

My son is hungry. Please. We came to ask for some leftover scraps from dinner. . . ."

The Frassatis were a wealthy family and their home was large, so it was not unusual for people in need to come asking for food or money. Mr. and Mrs. Frassati were out for the evening, and they had left Maria, a maid, to watch the children. She had fallen asleep in a chair.

Pier Giorgio invited this hungry and cold pair into the foyer and then ran to the kitchen. He and Luciana quickly packed up what was left of the dinner roast, some vegetables, and a loaf of bread.

"Shh, Luciana," warned Pier Giorgio. "We'll really be in trouble if Maria wakes up and finds us giving away the rest of our supper. But this family is in need and we have plenty to share."

As Pier Giorgio gave the sack of food to the woman, he glanced down and saw that the little boy was shifting from foot to foot because he was barefoot.

"My friend!" cried Pier Giorgio. "You need shoes! It's too cold for you to walk barefoot." Instantly, he bent down, pulled his own shoes off his feet, and handed them to the boy.

"Thank you," the boy whispered, almost too quietly to hear.

Pier Giorgio sent them off with well wishes and a blessing. As he closed the door, Luciana cried out, "What were you thinking? Mama and Papa will be furious. And what will you do without shoes for the winter?"

"I will ask Papa for some extra chores to earn money to buy new ones," answered Pier Giorgio. "And I will tell him that Jesus needed mine."

Pier Giorgio seemed to always be giving his things away to Jesus hidden in the faces of the poor. At seventeen years old, he joined the local Saint Vincent de Paul Society and began to give away the small amounts of spending money he received from his father. His parents gave him bus fare for traveling to and from school so that he would be home in time for dinner each evening. But instead of taking the bus, Pier Giorgio often gave his bus fare to the poor and then ran all the way home to avoid being late. When he traveled by train, he traveled in third class and gave the money he saved to the poor.

"Why do you travel in third class?" asked a classmate, scornfully.

"Because there is no fourth class," replied Pier Giorgio.

As a teenager, Pier Giorgio would often spend all-night vigils before the Blessed Sacrament, adoring Jesus in the Eucharist. These long nights of prayer filled him with the love of God and inspired him to share God's love with the poor of Turin.

Pier Giorgio performed countless acts of charity, but he also supported social reforms that would eliminate some of the need for charity. Popular and well-liked among his peers, Pier Giorgio led a group of his fellow students in a

1921 rally to protest a dictator's rise to power. Pier Giorgio and his friends marched with 50,000 other Italian Catholic Youth. They carried a large banner high over their heads. When the students reached the city square, the police began beating the protesters, tearing their flags and banners to pieces. Never one to run away from a challenge, Pier Giorgio grabbed one of the poles used to hold up the banner and began to fight back against the police in order to protect his fellow marchers.

Not surprisingly, Pier Giorgio and the other protesters were detained by the police in a nearby courtyard. As more familiar faces arrived, Pier Giorgio welcomed his friends and urged them to remain calm despite the mounting chaos and violence. Things reached a breaking point when one of the priests in the group was thrown to the ground and his cassock torn. The students were outraged and the fight began anew, with police waving their bayonets.

In an effort to halt the violence, Pier Giorgio shouted out the name of his wealthy and influential father, "Alfredo Frassati!" When he heard the name of the ambassador to Germany and owner of Turin's daily newspaper, the police lieutenant ordered his men to stop. Realizing whose son Pier Giorgio was, the lieutenant became courteous and polite. He even offered to release Pier Giorgio and allow him to go home. But Pier Giorgio refused; he would not leave his friends behind. It would be unjust to abandon his comrades in order to take advantage of his family's prominence. Instead, he sat down next to the injured priest, pulled out his rosary, and invited all those present to join him in praying not only for their cause, but also for the men who had attacked them.

Pier Giorgio was often praised for his courageous actions, but he believed that he was merely doing what was just. Frightened of the consequences of some of Pier Giorgio's political activities, his friends begged him to be careful. Pier Giorgio, however, would not back down. He knew that to hide silently out of cowardice would open wide the doors to tyrannical injustice.

When he was twenty-four years old, Pier Giorgio contracted polio. Less than a week after becoming ill, Pier Giorgio died. His funeral was packed with mourners. But they were not the people many expected to attend. Rather than just the wealthy members of Turin's upper class, the poor and needy people of the city came to his funeral by the thousands. Pier Giorgio's parents and their friends were shocked. They had no idea of the extent to which he had led a "secret life" of service. Those he had helped were also shocked because they didn't realize Pier Giorgio came from such a prominent, wealthy family. He never treated them as anything but his equals. In fact, he treated them as more than equals; he treated them as Jesus in disguise.

Because of Pier Giorgio's great love for God, he was able to live with great love for his fellow human beings. His personal motto was, "To the heights!" Rooted in a deep prayer life, Pier Giorgio's love of God and neighbor reached to the heights, as witnessed by the crowds that gathered to mourn his death.

Blessed Pier Giorgio Frassati was just because he gave his love and devotion first to God, then also worked to improve the lives of the poor and vulnerable.

Prayer for Justice

Dear God of Justice,
please help me to recognize the many gifts you have given to me and let me see the needs of others. Show me how to use my gifts to help them and honor you. Help me also to recognize the ways in which I have hurt others or failed to give them what they deserve. Give me the opportunity to right those wrongs. Let me always remember that every good gift comes from you and should be returned to you with gratitude. Amen.

How Can I Train to Be a Hero of Justice?

I can make a habit of thanking God each night for the gifts and blessings I have received during the day. What can I thank him for today?

Do I give God what I owe him? Is there someone I can ask for the support I need to attend Mass on Sundays and holy days of obligation? Or, is there someone I can offer to bring with me to Mass?

How is going to the Sacrament of Reconciliation and doing penance for my sins an act of justice?

What are some ways I can generously share my time, possessions, and talents with other people?

Is there something I did recently that hurt someone else? Did I admit my mistake and apologize quickly? What is the just thing for me to do to make things right now?

Chapter 3

29

Fortitude and Saints Peter Yu Tae-chol and Agatha Yi

What Is Fortitude?

Have you ever made a decision to do something difficult, like stand up for a classmate who is being bullied or excluded? When you first resolve to do this, you may be motivated and convinced of the rightness of your actions. Yet when the time comes to follow through, difficulties and temptations arise. Maybe your best friend is one of the bullies and you can't help but think how much easier it would be to remain silent than to challenge a friend. Or perhaps you do defend your classmate, but you instantly become another target of the bullies. Suddenly, you feel your commitment to doing the right thing slipping away. This is why we need fortitude!

"In the world you have faced persecution. But take courage; I have conquered the world!"
John 16:33

Sometimes we decide to make a change in our lives, like giving up sweets for Lent or making a New Year's resolution to keep our bedroom neat. At first, we are able to keep our resolution out of excitement and because it is something new. Eventually though, it becomes more difficult to wake up each morning and make the bed, or to turn down an offer of candy from a friend. Fortitude is what enables us to follow through on our commitments to do good when our enthusiasm dies down or when obstacles spring up in our path.

When Jesus had been fasting for forty days in the desert, Satan came to him and said, "If you are the Son of God, command these stones to become loaves of bread." After forty days of fasting, Jesus would have been ravenous! But his fortitude gave him the inner strength to rebuke Satan and reject his temptation. "One does not live by bread alone, but by every word that comes forth from the mouth of God," Jesus responded (Matthew 4:3–4). It was fortitude that enabled Jesus to complete his fast in order that he might draw closer to God his Father and prepare for his mission on earth.

When we face the things that scare us—like physical pain, suffering, or ridicule—fortitude gives us the strength to continue on the right path. Fortitude allows us to face our fears and the difficulties that sometimes come when we do what is right. Fortitude gives us the strength to do things we may not be able to do otherwise.

Who Are Saints Peter Yu Tae-chol and Agatha Yi?

Korea, during the 1830s

Growing up Catholic in Korea was very different from growing up as a Catholic anywhere else in the world. That is because the Church in Korea was founded and led entirely by lay people rather than missionary priests and religious. A Korean man, Yi Seung-hun, visited China with his father in 1783. In China, he met with a Catholic priest who taught him about the Gospel, and he decided to be baptized. When he returned to his Korean homeland, Yi Seung-hun brought his newfound Christian faith with him, and he shared it with others. The Church in Korea grew quickly.

The first Catholic priests arrived in Korea about forty years later, when Peter Yu Tae-chol and Agatha Yi were young children. By this time, Korean Catholics were already facing violent persecution by a government hostile to their faith. Like most of the Korean faithful, Peter and Agatha gathered each Sunday to worship God, read Scripture, and pray. There were no Masses, no Eucharist, no confessions or confirmations, however, because there were so few priests.

In the summer of 1839, Korean authorities were arresting, jailing, and killing Korean Christians. Peter's father, Augustine, was a devout Catholic who had worked as a translator for the Korean government. When government officials discovered that he was a Christian, they charged him with treason, imprisoned him, and killed him.

Inspired by his courageous father, Peter resisted the pleas of his non-Christian mother and sister to deny his faith in order to preserve his freedom. Although he was only thirteen, Peter stood in the middle of the courtroom, before a panel of Korean authorities, with his eyes cast down and his hands clasped behind his back.

"Why have you come here?" one of the tribunal members asked him.

"I have come to turn myself in. I am a Catholic," was his straightforward response. Peter's declaration was met with a stunned silence. Slowly, a sly smile spread across the face of one of the judges.

"Surely this is a mistake," the judge said. "Come now, be reasonable. I know it must have been very difficult to have a father who filled your head with this nonsense.

But I hope you've learned a lesson from him. Would your mother want you to meet the same end as your father? Executed for this Jesus? For nothing?"

Peter was unwavering. "I am a Catholic Christian," he repeated. At first, the tribunal continued trying to persuade him to deny his Catholic faith. Then they threatened him and beat him. Nothing would sway Peter in his faith and love for Christ.

"Take him to prison!" the judge finally ordered. "Nothing else can be done about this one. Soon he'll see his error."

Peter was imprisoned with adult Christians who also refused to deny Christ. Like them, he was subject to painful torture in the prison. It is said that he was whipped six hundred times.

"Do you still believe in God?" mocked the prison guard.

"Yes, I do," Peter responded, smiling.

Enraged, the guard shouted, "Shut your mouth or I will put a burning charcoal in it!"

"I am ready," said Peter, as he opened his mouth. Shamed by this young boy's unfailing courage and joy, the guard could not follow through with his threat. He turned away, muttering about the boy's disrespect and foolishness.

Peter escaped the burning charcoal that day, but he did not escape further suffering. He was questioned and tortured fourteen times during his imprisonment. Even though he was being brutally beaten, Peter remained calm. A smile never left his face. He repeated the words he had heard his own father speak, "Once having known God, I cannot possibly betray him."

◌◦◌

Agatha Yi, another Christian teen, had been imprisoned for several months. She and her brother were separated from their parents. The guards tortured the entire Yi family over long months, interrogating them again and again and demanding that they renounce their faith. Nevertheless, the Yis remained steadfast.

"Your parents have already renounced this Christ you speak of," the guards told Agatha. In fact, their parents had remained loyal to Christ and his Church. The guards had lied because they thought Agatha would lose courage if she believed her parents had abandoned Christianity. They underestimated Agatha's fortitude.

Agatha's only response was, "Whether or not my parents denied their faith is their choice. As for us, we cannot betray the Lord of heaven, whom we have always served."

Upon hearing Agatha's courageous proclamation of faith, six adult prisoners willingly accepted martyrdom. For the next nine months, Agatha was beaten, starved, and tortured in retaliation. Much like Peter, Agatha found strength in the example set by her parents, both of whom died for their faith in the Korean prison.

Agatha and Peter's unfailing courage in the face of ridicule and torture convinced the guards that neither would ever deny their faith. In fact, Peter went so far as to call out fellow Catholics who were imprisoned with him. One man faltered in his commitment to Christianity as he suffered under the pressures of torture and abuse. Peter admonished him, "You are a catechist and a grown man. I am only a boy. You are the one who ought to be helping me to suffer courageously. How is it that we have changed places?"

Resolute in their own determination to rid Korea of Christianity, the authorities decided to have Peter, Agatha, and many others killed to put an end to the example and inspiration they provided for their fellow Christians. Peter and Agatha were both strangled to death; Peter in the fall of 1839 and Agatha just a few months later in January of 1840.

Saints Peter and Agatha were certainly afraid of the danger they faced. Their own parents had been martyred and they knew that they, too, would probably be killed for their faith. But fortitude gave both teens the strength to be faithful witnesses to the love of Jesus. Because of their heroic witness of faith in the face of imprisonment, torture, and even death, both Peter and Agatha are among the 10,000 Korean Christian martyrs of their century. They also belong to the group of 103 Korean Martyrs later canonized by Pope John Paul II.

Saints Peter Yu Tae-chol and Agatha Yi showed fortitude when they bravely faced torture and martyrdom for their faith rather than deny Jesus.

● ●

Prayer for Fortitude

Dear God of Strength,
when I am scared or weak, help me to remember to call on you. When I make a decision to do good, and then begin to doubt myself or feel my commitment fading, give me the gift of fortitude. When I am frustrated and struggling, keep me from giving up. Give me your strength and endurance in the face of every obstacle and temptation. Amen.

How Can I Train to Be a Hero of Fortitude?

When something is painful or embarrassing, what can I do to offer my discomfort or suffering to God?

When a task, job, or activity becomes difficult or is no longer interesting, what can I do to respond with fortitude?

When someone else is doing the right thing in a difficult situation, how can I encourage them?

What is a quotation, song, or image that encourages me not to give up, and where could I put a copy of it so that I will encounter it every day?

What is an example of a time I can ask God to help me to remain strong? What kinds of things make me frightened, tired, or feel like I am losing hope?

Chapter 4

Temperance and Venerable Matt Talbot

What Is Temperance?

Temperance helps us to prioritize things by determining their importance. It also teaches us how to enjoy, consume, and use things *appropriately*. When John's disciples demanded to know why they and the Pharisees fasted, but Jesus' disciples did not, Jesus responded, "The wedding guests cannot mourn as long as the bridegroom is with them, can they? The days will come when the bridegroom is taken away from them, and then they will fast" (Matthew 9:15). Jesus taught his questioners that there is a time for everything. Sometimes it is appropriate to fast, and sometimes it is appropriate to feast. Temperance teaches us when it is time for feasting

> . . . live lives that
> are self-controlled,
> upright, and godly, while
> we wait for the blessed hope
> and the manifestation of the
> glory of our great God and
> Savior, Jesus Christ.
>
> Titus 2:12–13

and when it is time for fasting. It helps us find the balance.

Our world is filled with good gifts from God. We experience God in people we love, such as our family and friends. We also experience God in beautiful places, happy memories, special objects, and even our favorite foods. All these good things are like little signs pointing us to God.

Think about when you go on a long car ride or road trip with your family. When you first get on the highway, you check the signs to make sure you are heading in the right direction. As the names of other places between your home and your final destination begin to appear on signs, you know that you are making progress. Eventually, you start to see signs with the name of your destination and exactly how many more miles you have left to go.

When you see the first road sign with the name of your final destination on it, do you stop the car, jump out, grab the sign, and just hang out there? Of course not! The sign isn't your goal; it is just there to point you in the right direction so you reach your final destination.

Sometimes it is hard for us to remember that the good things of earth are just *signs*. It's easy to mistake them for our final goal, especially when we're enjoying them. When we make this mistake, we sometimes end up learning that too much of a good thing isn't good at all. Have you ever eaten too much cake and ice cream at a birthday party? Afterward, you probably had a stomachache. Have your eyes ever been bigger than your stomach? Then you may have ended up throwing away something you probably shouldn't have taken in the first place.

Of course, this doesn't mean that you should never enjoy a treat; it just means that we need to practice *temperance*, or avoid excesses and wastefulness. If we don't eat enough, we will starve. If we eat too much, we will get sick, perhaps seriously. If we have the virtue of temperance, we avoid unhealthy extremes. We allow God's gifts here on earth to point us to his ultimate gift, instead of being a distraction. Temperance helps us to balance our enjoyment of these earthly "signs" with the goodness of our true destination: heaven!

Who Is Venerable Matt Talbot?

Ireland, during the 1880s

Matt stood outside O'Meara's Pub on a warm afternoon in the summer of 1884. He searched the crowded Dublin street for familiar faces. The nagging headache that was a result of last night's trip to the pub hung on. Nonetheless, a wry smile crossed Matt's face as he thought of how he and his brothers had swiped a fiddle from a street musician and pawned it for money. They'd used the money to buy drinks for everyone in the pub. They'd even bought a drink for the fiddle player, who hadn't yet realized his fiddle was missing. When he discovered the missing instrument, he was less than amused. *Ah well. It had been a great evening,* thought Matt. *I'm sure the fellow managed to work things out somehow.*

Matt remembered his headache again and thought that if he could just get a drink, he'd feel better. But he was completely out of money until next payday and had no more credit at the pub. If a friend would just spot him the money for the next few days, he thought, he'd pay the friend back when he got paid. A couple of his buddies approached the door, and Matt took his hat in hand and gave them a sheepish grin. But before he could ask to borrow money, they ducked inside the door, avoiding conversation. *No matter, someone else will be along in a moment*, he thought. A small band of young men Matt knew came along, laughing and joking.

"Hi lads! I was wondering—" But Matt was cut off as the men refused to make eye contact and rushed into the pub. This scene repeated itself several times as friends and acquaintances arrived. All of them avoided speaking to Matt as they entered the pub.

Well, thought Matt. *This is a fine fix to be in. Even my best friends won't speak to me. No one to lend me a bit of money for a drink and not a penny to my name until payday.* Matt knew, too, that most of his next paycheck really belonged to others whom he'd already borrowed money from in order to pay for his drinking.

Matt had nowhere to go but home. Walking across the Newcomen Bridge, something happened. For the first time in his life, Matt saw the reality of his situation. He had wasted his life. All of his drinking buddies and good-time friends avoided him when he couldn't afford to join them in the pub. None were actually interested in him as a person. He was penniless and friendless. Humiliated and disgusted with himself, Matt felt ashamed. In that moment, he became determined to change.

When Matt arrived home, his mother was preparing supper. Mrs. Talbot looked up, surprised to see Matt home, early and sober, on a Saturday.

"Mum, I've decided to take the pledge," he announced to her. "I'm going to make a solemn promise to stay away from alcohol." Matt's mother was shocked. At first she wasn't sure what to think or say.

"Matt, taking an oath before God isn't a joke. You must be serious! You mustn't do it on a whim!"

"I know, Mum. I'm quite serious," Matt said.

Then Matt walked to Holy Cross College, where he knelt in the confessional and confessed his sins. After confessing and receiving absolution, Matt pledged to abstain from alcohol and remain sober. Freed from the burden of his sins, Matt attended Mass the next morning and received Holy Communion for the first time in years.

Matt had been drinking for sixteen years. In fact, he'd had his first drink before he was even thirteen years old. By the age of sixteen, he was a confirmed alcoholic. Matt had pawned his belongings, including his clothes and shoes, in order to get more money for drinking. He'd run up large debts in many pubs and spent all his evening and weekend hours drinking with friends. It wouldn't be easy to stop altogether now just because he'd taken the pledge, and Matt knew it. He needed a plan—and the grace of God— if he was to succeed.

Matt resolved to begin each day by attending morning Mass at 5:00 am. There, he would receive Jesus in the

Eucharist and ask Jesus to protect him from temptation throughout the day. After work, when his friends went to a pub to drink, Matt planned to disappear into a church somewhere and pray. For the first week, Matt's plan worked perfectly. He rose early, attended Mass, worked all day at the lumberyards, and then slipped away to some distant church where he knelt in prayer until it was time to go home to dinner and bed.

On Saturday, however, Matt's strength was tested. He was unable to disappear quietly as the work day ended and his pals teased him about his absence during the previous week. Not wanting to offend anyone, Matt joined them at a local pub. He drank only water, but the temptation to drink alcohol with his friends was overwhelming. Afterward, Matt decided he would never enter the pub again. For him, just being there was a great temptation to break his pledge to stay sober.

Matt knew that he needed God's grace to strengthen him in the face of temptation. But he also knew that he needed to avoid temptations in the first place. Matt's frequent visits to church helped him with both; he prayed before the tabernacle to be faithful to his promise, and his prayer time gave him a place to be other than in a pub.

Before taking the pledge, Matt was enslaved to alcohol. His early years were filled with overindulgence in alcohol and all the problems that come with that: poverty, poor health, damaged relationships, and family suffering. The virtue of temperance set Matt free. No longer did his entire life revolve around drinking. No longer was every penny he earned immediately spent in Dublin's pubs.

Instead, Matt was able to contribute to his family and cultivate relationships and friendships with people who valued him for the person he was. At work, he became known for being honest, industrious, and devout. When Matt heard the other men in the yard curse or tell crude jokes, he would say a silent prayer and bow his head briefly. At times, he took younger men aside and encouraged them not to laugh at these kinds of stories and jokes. His example was so positive that eventually the others stopped cursing when they were in his presence.

Still, nobody considered Matt Talbot a Goody Two-shoes or spoilsport. He liked a good story and laughed at funny jokes. Matt's love for Jesus and the Church grew and he read voraciously—Scripture, the lives of the saints, and other spiritual reading. He often lent his books out to friends and spent evenings talking with them about what he was reading. Matt even tried to find and repay the fiddler whose fiddle he and his brothers had stolen years before. Unable to find him, Matt took the money and had Masses offered for the man instead.

Matt's first few years without alcohol presented nearly constant temptation to return to drinking. Matt faced this challenge day by day, and he succeeded in remaining sober for the rest of his life. Without the distraction of drinking, Matt discovered the love of Christ when he needed God the most. Ultimately, he realized that the true happiness he had been seeking in alcohol, he could find only in God. Matt was an ordinary worker from a poor Irish family, yet he did the extraordinary through God's grace and the virtue of temperance. He is a witness to the power of virtue to make ordinary people heroes.

Venerable Matt Talbot
showed temperance
when he quit drinking, turned away
from a life of addiction, and made
a commitment to staying sober.

● ●

Prayer for Temperance

Dear God of All Goodness,
help me to recognize the goodness of everything and everyone you have made. Show me how to enjoy what you have
created and given me in healthy and balanced ways. Help me
to always remember that of all that is good, you are the best.
Give me the grace to be able to set good things aside for better
things and the wisdom to choose what will lead me to heaven.
Amen.

How Can I Train to Be a Hero of Temperance?

Can I take "no" for an answer? When was the last time I chose to "say no" to myself? What did I say "no" to?

Is there something good that I am often tempted to overuse, overdo, over-consume, or waste? What are examples of some small sacrifices I can make to practice temperance?

Instead of always trying to get more "stuff," what can I do to remind myself to be satisfied with the good things I already have?

It is important to pray, work, play, and rest each day. What could I do to better balance the way I spend my time?

How can I use my time, money, and talents more moderately?

Part II

The Theological Virtues

If you went on a long camping trip, you would pack food, water, clothing, a tent, and other supplies. The theological virtues are the supplies of faith, hope, and love that the Holy Spirit has packed for us. They aren't things that we can pack for ourselves. They are, however, the virtues we need to sustain us through life here on earth as we journey toward eternal life with God in heaven.

Like the cardinal virtues, the theological virtues are habits that allow us to live holy lives. But unlike the cardinal virtues, they are not qualities or habits we can

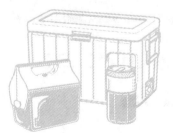

develop on our own. The theological virtues are given to us as the pure gift of God at Baptism. *Theos*, in fact, means "God." The theological virtues help us to live as the children of God, and they prepare us to live with God forever in heaven. We receive them when we receive the Holy Spirit and become the

we reach our final destination: heaven.

The theological virtues are free gifts from God, but we have a responsibility to make good use of them. That's where the cardinal, or human, virtues come in! For example, if we are prudent, we are able to discern the best way to share and show our faith, even when it's difficult. When we receive God's free gift of the theological virtues and accept the help of the Holy Spirit to develop the cardinal virtues, we reflect God's goodness and become his heroes in the world.

adoptive children of God. God gives us the theological virtues so that we are able to become more like him. Like supplies you bring with you on a camping trip, they are things we need on the journey of life. The theological virtues are part of God's promise to be with us and guide us on our journey until

Chapter 5

Faith and Lucia dos Santos, Blessed Francisco Marto and Blessed Jacinta Marto
The Children of Fatima

What Is Faith?

Faith is a gift. We say we have faith when we believe what God has "told" us about himself. God reveals himself to us in many ways. Among them are creation, the Church, the Bible, the sacraments, and the lives of the saints. But faith is even more than *what* we believe; it has to do with *who* we believe. People of faith trust God with their lives and place everything in his hands. If we have faith, we commit ourselves to seeking to know God's truth and carrying out his will in our lives.

As Jesus traveled to the city of Jericho, a blind beggar sitting by the side of the road

> "... if you have faith the size of a mustard seed, you will say to this mountain, 'Move from here to there,' and it will move; and nothing will be impossible for you."
>
> Matthew 17:20

shouted out to him, "Jesus, Son of David, have mercy on me!" The crowd shushed him, but the blind man continued to call out to Jesus.

Hearing his plea, Jesus said, "Receive your sight; your faith has saved you." The blind man was healed and followed Jesus, praising God (see Luke 18:35–43). Not only did his faith allow Jesus to heal him, it also served as an example to the others around him, whose own faith grew because of his example.

Have you learned about dinosaurs in school? Or the planets of our solar system? What about a historical figure like Alexander Graham Bell? It's very likely that you've seen illustrations of dinosaurs

or models and learned about the food they ate. You can probably describe the attributes of different planets, even though you've never traveled there. And, if you were asked what Alexander Graham Bell's most significant contribution was, you might say he invented the telephone.

But none of us have ever seen a dinosaur, since they became extinct long before our time. We haven't traveled to Neptune to see firsthand what it is like. Because Alexander Graham Bell died many years before we were born, we have never personally met him.

So how can you know about a person or thing or place if you have no firsthand experience? You were taught these things by a trustworthy person who had the knowledge, skills, and authority to teach you. That person shared information about the subject by providing specific examples and evidence. For example, when your class studied dinosaurs, your teacher might have explained about the work of paleontologists and how they use artifacts like fossils to get an idea of what different types of dinosaurs looked like and what they ate.

Faith in God works in a similar way. Although we can experience God in many ways and be close to him in prayer, God doesn't usually talk to us directly in a voice we can hear with our ears. Instead, God gives us the gift of his Church, who is like a mother and teacher to us on earth. The Church tells us beautiful truths about God and his love for us. She shows us how we can know these things and helps us to understand them. Having faith doesn't mean that we never question, doubt, disagree, or think for ourselves. What it does mean is that we accept God's truth as *the* truth, and are willing to work through the challenges. Faith is embracing these truths and trying to live our lives in a way that reflects them.

The gift of faith is given to us by God at our Baptism. It is a gift that comes with a big responsibility: the mission to share it. We are called to bring the message of the Gospel to everyone we meet. Jesus told his Apostles to share their faith with the whole world and to make disciples of all nations. We do this when we share our faith with our family, at school, or on a sports team. Sharing our faith is part of living our life in a way that shows that we believe God—and believe in him.

Who Are Lucia, Blessed Francisco, and Blessed Jacinta?

Portugal, in 1917

Ten-year-old Lucia dos Santos and her younger cousins Francisco and Jacinta Marto sat down on the side of the hill outside their hometown of Fatima and unpacked their lunch. It was a warm and sunny May afternoon in 1917. World War I was being fought on battlefields across Europe. In the fields outside the tiny Portuguese village of Fatima, however, all was peaceful. Spring flowers bloomed in abundance beneath the cloudless sky, and the church bells tolled distantly from the center of the village. The flock of sheep were grazing nearby, and the shepherd children were tired and hungry from leading them all out to pasture.

"We haven't said our Rosary yet," seven-year-old Jacinta reminded them. Francisco, pretending not to hear her, pulled his wooden flute out of his knapsack and began playing. "We have to say our Rosary!" Jacinta insisted. "Mama said so." She pouted when her nine-year-old brother and cousin both ignored her.

"Alright, alright," sighed Lucia. "But let's just say a shortcut Rosary instead."

"Shortcut Rosary?"

"Yes, you just say the names of the prayers, 'Our Father, Hail Mary . . .' instead of saying *all* the words."

After saying their prayers and eating lunch, the children began a game of building a tiny house of stones and twigs harvested from the pasture. Francisco gave directions on the building process and sent Lucia and Jacinta to fetch more materials. The children were laughing and having fun with the construction of their little house when they were suddenly interrupted.

Crack! Lightning flashed across the sky and the children quickly gathered up their belongings and began to round up the sheep to drive them down the hill toward home. Another flash of light illuminated the sky and all three children ducked under their shawls, expecting rain to pour from the sky.

When the rain did not come, Lucia lifted her head and saw an amazing sight. A beautiful lady dressed in white stood near them; light streamed from her body.

"Oh look!" whispered Lucia. Jacinta and Francisco looked up and gasped.

"Please don't be afraid. I won't hurt you. I come from

heaven." The woman was so gentle and loving that the children's fears melted.

"Why are you here? Do you want something from us?" asked Lucia.

"I want you to pray the Rosary every day, to pray for peace and an end to war." The light began to fade and the lady disappeared, but not before promising that she would return to visit the children again the following month.

The children decided not to tell anyone what they had seen, but Jacinta accidentally revealed their secret to her mother. Thinking Jacinta's story was cute, her mother began sharing her daughter's story with her friends and relatives. The story spread around the small village rather quickly. Some wondered if something miraculous was happening. Most thought it was innocent child's play. Even their parish priest, Father Ferreira, suggested, "All children make up stories for attention. They'll forget about this soon enough."

Others, however, were angry, and they accused the children of lying. Lucia's mother asked her daughter about it. Lucia told her what the three children had seen, but her mother did not believe her. She begged Lucia not to mention it ever again and warned that she would be punished severely if she did not obey.

The lady from heaven kept her promise and appeared to the children on the thirteenth day of each month. The three young shepherds did their best to do what the lady asked of them. After a few months of controversy in the village, Mayor Arturo Santos, who did not believe in God, decided to take action. He had all three children arrested and put into the town jail. At first the children were frightened. The oldest of the three of them, after all, was only ten years old, and they had been locked up with adult criminals.

Lucia reminded Francisco and Jacinta, "Our Lady told us that the Rosary is a very powerful prayer. Let's pray our rosaries here and invite the other prisoners to join us." Their fellow prisoners were inspired by the faith of these young children and actually *did* join them in praying. This further infuriated Mayor Arturo Santos, who certainly did not expect criminals to respond to the faith of children.

"I will put an end to this," he vowed. All three children were taken to a small room to be questioned. "Admit that you have lied about seeing this lady!" demanded the mayor. "Confess to your deceit and I will release you."

"But sir," Lucia said softly, "we cannot confess. We really did see her. We aren't lying!"

"Do you wish to be boiled in a pot of oil? Because that is what will happen to you if you do not admit your guilt!"

"No, sir. But we won't confess to something we haven't done. We have not told any lies." Finally, the mayor gave up in frustration and sent them home to their families.

Sadly for Lucia, Francisco, and Jacinta, some of their siblings and friends mocked them when they returned home. Despite the cruel way some others treated them, the three children stuck to their story, prayed the Rosary every day, and offered up their sufferings as sacrifices for the conversion of sinners. Surrounded by people who did not believe them, the children put their faith in God.

Our Lady made her last appearance in Fatima in October. On that day, about 70,000 people had gathered in the field where the Blessed Mother had visited the children. They came even in the pouring rain because they had heard that the lady from heaven had promised Lucia that she would perform a miracle. Some of the crowd believed that the Blessed Virgin Mary was going to appear, while others wondered. Still others were convinced that the whole thing was a hoax.

The children had said the lady would appear at midday. As noon came and went, the crowd began to jeer. Despite the ridicule, Lucia insisted that Our Lady would keep her promise. Shortly after one o'clock, the children knelt as the Blessed Virgin Mary appeared. She instructed the children to continue praying the Rosary every day and to tell the priests to have a chapel built where she had appeared to them. Lucia asked the beautiful lady her name, and she at last revealed it: Our Lady of the Rosary.

Only the three children saw the Blessed Mother. But the entire crowd of thousands witnessed what happened next. Suddenly, the sun danced in the sky and sent a rain-

bow of colors streaming through the air. Then it began to spin as if it was going to crash to the earth. People screamed with fear. The muddy fields and the people's rain-soaked clothing dried immediately in the light of the spinning sun. The effect was so stunning that newspapers all over the world reported the event, calling it the "Miracle of the Sun." That day, many people came to believe that the message of prayer and conversion shared by Lucia, Jacinta, and Francisco was true.

The Blessed Virgin Mary came to the children of Fatima six times. Her visits changed the lives and hearts of Lucia, Francisco, and Jacinta. Because they had experienced how much the Blessed Mother loved them and wanted to bring them to her Son, Jesus, the three children no longer thought of prayer as a chore. Instead, they experienced it as a privilege and something they could do to help bring peace to the world.

Our Lady also asked the children to offer small sacrifices for the conversion of sinners. Whenever something unpleasant happened, like running out of drinking water on a hot day in the fields with their sheep, the children would offer their discomfort to Jesus as a sacrifice instead of complaining. They would pray, "Oh Jesus, this is out of love for you and for the conversion of sinners."

Lucia, Jacinta, and Francisco believed what the Blessed Mother told them about God's love and his desire for us to live with him in heaven forever. They trusted that Mary would lead them to God. The children did not just *say* they believed; they made choices that *showed* their belief. They prayed every day, stood up for the truth even when they were mocked or accused of lying, and continued to grow closer to God and follow his will for them.

Blesseds Jacinta and Francisco Marto and their cousin Lucia dos Santos chose to live their faith when they believed the message the Blessed Mother spoke to them and lived their lives according to it.

Prayer for Faith

Dear God of All,
I believe that you are real and that you love me. Give me the grace to trust you even more than I already do. Be with me when I struggle or doubt. I know that my life should be a witness to your love. Help me to live in a way that shows how much I believe in you. Show me how to bring my faith to others. Amen.

How Can I Train to Be a Hero of Faith?

What are some things I do now that show my faith? Is there something else I could add to what I already do?

How might I help younger children in my family, school, or parish to grow in their faith?

What "message" of faith could I share with others?

What questions do I have about my faith? What can I do if I experience doubt?

Have I been able to stand up for what I believe even if it isn't popular? What—or who—could help me?

71

Hope and Saint Josephine Bakhita

What Is Hope?

Have you ever said, "I hope I get the teacher I want," or, "I hope my team wins the game"? We often say we *hope* something will happen when we are really talking about wishes. We *wish* we would be assigned to our favorite teacher and we *wish* our team would win. These are good things we want to happen even though we aren't sure if they will. But the virtue of hope is different.

Hope is more than just wishing for something. Hope can be compared to the way we count down until Christmas morning, or look forward to a delicious meal when we are really hungry, or a warm house when it is freezing cold outside. It is

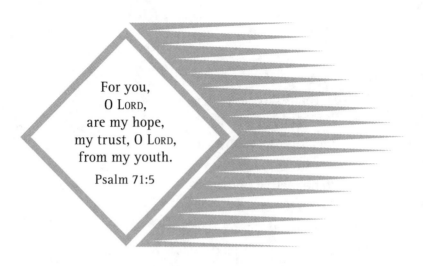

For you,
O LORD,
are my hope,
my trust, O LORD,
from my youth.

Psalm 71:5

longing for something you know is real and simply isn't "here" *yet*.

Even on the Cross on Good Friday, Jesus remained hopeful. When the criminal at his side begged, "Jesus, remember me when you come into your kingdom," Jesus promised him that, "today you will be with me in Paradise" (Luke 23:42–43). Jesus knew then, as he always had, that heaven is real and that his death on the Cross would bring salvation to sinners.

We are hopeful when we trust that God will keep his word to us and honor the promise he made to save us. Hope gives us the long view of things. It reassures us that no matter what troubles we encounter, Jesus offers us eternal life in heaven, where we will be perfectly happy forever. Thanks to our faith in what God has revealed to us, hope helps us to wait confidently for the good things we know to be real. Hopeful people rely on God's grace to eventually bring them, and others, every good thing he has promised us.

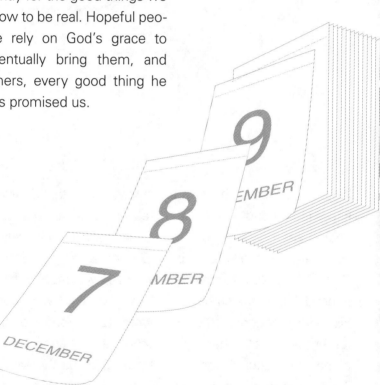

Who Is Saint Josephine Bakhita?

Sudan, in 1877

"What is your name?" demanded the strange man as he roughly jerked the nine-year-old girl's arm. Tears and terror filled the girl's wide eyes. She stood trembling in silence, unable to answer. The man sighed in irritation and said, "Fine, we'll call you Bakhita then!" All the other men burst into laughter. They were amused that a girl who had been kidnapped as she picked herbs in the Sudanese fields would be called by a name that meant *lucky*.

It was 1877, and Arab slave traders regularly captured Africans from their homes and villages to be sold into slavery at auctions and markets. Along with others who had been taken captive, Bakhita was forced to walk 600 miles to the city of El Obeid. There she was bought and sold as a slave five separate times.

Just a child, Bakhita, alone and without parents or family, was moved from house to house. The wife of Bakhita's fourth owner, a Turkish general, decided to tattoo all her slaves. She hired a woman to carefully draw 114 designs on Bakhita's chest, stomach, arms, and legs with flour and then cut the lines of the design into her skin with a razor blade.

"Lay still, Bakhita!" commanded her mistress. "Now I will rub salt into the wounds so that you will have scars and I can always see the beautiful design drawn on you." As she massaged the salt into Bakhita's tender flesh, the pain was almost unbearable. *I am going to die from pain. This cruelty is not right*, Bakhita thought, as she tried not to cry out. Bakhita knew that as a slave there was no one she could ask for help.

In an effort to keep herself from sinking into despair, Bakhita made a mental catalog of the beauty and goodness she had experienced in her life. When she looked at the stars and moon in the night sky, Bakhita asked herself who could have created such beauty. She longed to meet and know this great Master. Though she suffered greatly at the hands of her owners, Bakhita held on to hope in the good Master of the universe. This hope helped her to bear her pain and avoid bitterness.

At fourteen years old, Bakhita was sold once again. Her fifth owner was an Italian family living in Sudan. Bakhita soon became the nanny for the Michieli family's daughter, Mimmina. Bakhita accompanied Mimmina to a boarding school run by the Canossian sisters in Venice, Italy. While she was there, Bakhita heard of God the Father and his great love for his people for the very first time. She learned about God's Son, Jesus, who had died to save people from their sins; and the Holy Spirit who lived in the hearts of believers.

The Canossian sisters introduced Bakhita to the Church and the sacraments. Many things she had not understood before began to make sense. At last Bakhita had met the God whom she had experienced in her heart since her childhood in the Sudan. The sun, moon, and stars had long ago pointed Bakhita to God, their Creator, but Bakhita had never before received any kind of religious education. Now she finally knew who God was. She also knew it was he who had sustained her through every abuse she had suffered.

Bakhita was anything but "lucky" when slave traders kidnapped her as a young girl. But the name given to her by slave traders turned out to be prophetic. When she arrived in Venice, Bakhita found that more than "lucky," she was blessed. God had brought her to a place where she would meet him, her true heavenly Master, who had walked beside her all this way, through fear and pain and loneliness.

One afternoon, Signora Michieli arrived at the school in Venice. Bakhita and Mimmina went out to the parlor to

meet her. "It is time for us to leave," she declared. "We are going to return to Sudan. Get your things packed this evening and in the morning we will head home."

Bakhita took a deep breath and gathered her courage. "Signora Michieli, I am sorry, but I cannot return with you. I must stay here with the sisters. They have taught me about our Lord and his Church. I want to be baptized and become a religious sister." There was a moment of stunned silence. Furious, Signora Michieli approached the cardinal patriarch of Venice and demanded that he command Bakhita to return to the Michieli's home.

"Signora, I cannot do that. Slavery is illegal in Italy, as you know. Here, Bakhita is a free woman. She may choose to continue working for you or not. But you may not force her to accompany you," Cardinal Agostini said.

After years of being enslaved, Bakhita was finally free to serve only her true Master, Jesus. Like Bakhita, Jesus had also suffered pain and loneliness. He understood and loved her completely. He was the one she had hoped for her entire life. *I am loved*, Bakhita thought. *No matter what happens, God is Love, and Love is waiting for me.* Jesus, her great hope, had redeemed her and set her free.

Cardinal Agostini baptized Bakhita when she was twenty years old. She took Josephine as her baptismal name. She became a consecrated Canossian sister six years later. As a Canossian sister, Bakhita longed to be a missionary in Africa. Her heart's desire was to return to her homeland and bring the joy of Christ, the Good Master, to the people there. But it was not to be. Bakhita served God as a doorkeeper, a seamstress, a cook, and set up for Mass in her convent. She was never able to travel back to her homeland as a missionary.

Ultimately, however, Bakhita's hope was fulfilled in a beautiful way. When Pope Saint John Paul II beatified her in 1992, he returned to Africa with her relics and encouraged the Sudanese people to rejoice that their native daughter, Bakhita, had returned to her homeland as a woman free in Christ.

Saint Josephine Bakhita placed her hope in a God she did not yet know as she suffered slavery and abuse. God fulfilled her hopes by setting her free and giving her the opportunity to know, love, and serve him.

Prayer for Hope

Dear God of Hope,
fill me with the assurance that your promises
will be fulfilled. Help me to see myself and
every person in my life as your beloved child,
made for heaven. Give me the grace I need to
persevere even through difficult times. Keep
me from turning to bitterness and despair.
Show me that I can always trust and rely
upon you, no matter what. Amen.

How Can I Train to Be a Hero of Hope?

God made me, and everyone else, to live with him in heaven forever. How can the hope of eternal life make my life here and now better?

How can I bring hope to my family, parish, and school?

What is something I *wish* for? What is something I *hope* for?

When things don't go the way I'd like, what can I do to keep from losing hope or becoming bitter?

When others hurt me or make me angry, how can I show particular kindness to them and ask God to help me forgive them?

Chapter 7

Love and Blessed Chiara Badano

What Is Love?

The word "love" can be very confusing. We say that we *love* sleeping in on Saturday mornings, we *love* chocolate ice cream, and we *love* our grandparents. But those "loves" are not at all the same. For Christians, perfect love, also called charity, is the greatest of all the virtues. Someone who loves God and others well always practices the rest of the virtues, too. That is because love is the source of all virtues, as well as their goal. We can be holy only because God loves us; we want to be holy because we love God in return.

God loves every one of us and wants only good for each person. When we are baptized, God comes to live in us

"You shall love the Lord your God with all your heart, and with all your soul, and with all your strength, and with all your mind; and your neighbor as yourself." Luke 10:27

in a unique way. We are brought to the baptismal font as God's creatures, made in his image. We leave the font as God's own children, adopted by the Heavenly Father himself. God gives his grace and love to us as free gifts, and he sends the Holy Spirit to enable us to love God and the people around us.

Perhaps you remember a sibling or cousin when he or she was a brand new baby. Did you notice how the baby's parents took such gentle care of the baby, feeding and diapering and rocking the baby, even if the baby fussed and cried? Or perhaps you've had a puppy or kitten. Did you mind playing with your new pet, cleaning up after it, or feeding it? Probably not, because when we love others, we want to show them

our love, even if the one we love has no way of thanking us or returning the favor.

Jesus gave his followers a new commandment: "love one another as I have loved you." He then explained what it means to love one another: "No one has greater love than this, to lay down one's life for one's friends" (John 15:12–13). Loving means giving ourselves, even if it is uncomfortable or inconvenient, because we want what is best for the person we love. We are most like God when we love someone in that way because God *is* love.

Who Is Blessed Chiara Badano?

Italy, in 1975

Chiara laid on the kitchen floor with toys she had recently received for her fourth birthday spread all around her.

"Vroom!" she said, as she crashed a toy truck into a tower of blocks. Chiara laughed as the blocks fell to the floor around her.

"Chiara, you have lots of toys," observed her mom.

"Yes, lots. So?"

"Maybe we could go choose some to give to poor children who have none," her mother gently suggested.

"But they are *mine*!" shouted Chiara, her eyes filling with tears. Frantically, she began to gather her toys into her arms and ran into the next room with them. For several minutes, Chiara's mom could hear hiccuping sobs in the next room. After a while, Chiara got quiet. Chiara's mom paused near the doorway, listening carefully.

Then she heard Chiara quietly talking to herself, saying, "This one yes, this one no." Peaking around the corner, Chiara's mom saw the toys divided into two piles. "Mommy, can you bring me a bag?" asked Chiara.

When Chiara's mother returned, she watched as Chiara put the toys from one of the large piles into the bag. "Chiara, those are your *new* toys!" exclaimed her mother.

"Mommy, I cannot give the old and broken toys to poor children who have nothing! That would be terrible." Chiara's eyes shone with tears once more, but unlike a few moments ago, these were tears of love for children who had nothing.

As Chiara grew, her love grew too. Chiara often showed her love for Jesus, as well as her family and friends, in many small and ordinary ways. One year, Chiara and her mother were preparing the table for their Christmas dinner.

"Please, Mom, can we use our most beautiful tablecloth?" Chiara pleaded. "Jesus will be with us today!" Chiara's love for Jesus was the source of her love for others. When a friend was sick with chicken pox, other children wouldn't visit her for fear of catching it. But Chiara risked getting sick and went to her friend so she wouldn't be alone. When asked if she was afraid of catching the disease, she declared, "Love is more important than fear."

As a teenager, Chiara excelled at sports, especially tennis. When she was seventeen, Chiara was playing tennis with a friend one summer afternoon when she felt a sharp pain shoot through her shoulder.

"Ouch!" she cried, dropping her racket on the ground. Her shoulder hurt too much to continue playing, so Chiara told her friend that they would have to finish their game another time, and she headed home. Chiara's mother was worried about her and took her to the doctor. The doctor ran some tests and discovered that the pain in Chiara's shoulder wasn't the result of an injury. She had a deadly form of bone cancer called osteosarcoma.

When Chiara first found out that she was very ill, she felt frightened and angry. She asked her mother not to talk to her right away. In this moment, Chiara realized that she had a choice between love and fear. Despite her anxiety, Chiara knew that she could turn her life into a gift of love for Jesus. Chiara decided to trust God and love him.

She prayed silently. *Jesus, please help me be brave. Help me say yes to you no matter what suffering comes my way. Help me to love you through it all.* Finishing her silent prayer, Chiara opened her eyes and said, "It's all right now, Mom and Dad. I have told Jesus yes. That because I love him, I want whatever he wants."

Chiara was admitted to the hospital for cancer treatment in 1988. There she underwent several surgeries and chemotherapy. The treatment, however, was not successful and Chiara's condition continued to worsen. Instead of complaining or feeling sorry for herself, Chiara spent her time with another teenage girl who was also in the hospital. The girl was addicted to drugs and very depressed. Chiara did not focus on her own pain, but instead took time to walk and talk with the girl so that she would not feel alone or abandoned. Eventually, Chiara's cancer progressed to the point that she could no longer walk. She told her mother that she would rather give up walking if it meant she would go to heaven.

The doctors wanted Chiara to take medicine that would relieve her pain, but Chiara refused because it made her feel tired and disoriented. Chiara knew she was dying, and she wanted to be able to offer her suffering to Jesus. She wanted to tell Jesus how much she loved him until the last minute of her life. Though she had almost nothing left, Chiara explained, she was still capable of love.

In her last days, Chiara helped her Mom plan her funeral. Chiara's parents were devastated that their bright, loving daughter would soon die. Chiara comforted her mother, telling her that when it was time for the funeral she must not be too sad, but should instead tell herself that Chiara was with Jesus. Chiara requested she be buried in a white dress, because she wanted to look like a bride going to meet her beloved Jesus. During her long illness, even when she felt tired or in pain, Chiara never missed an opportunity to love Jesus and the people around her.

Chiara's great love for God allowed her to see God in the people she met and to give all she had for others. In her suffering, the love Chiara had shown returned to

her. Many friends came to stay for hours with her in the hospital. Her friend Chicca reported that although she and others went to Chiara to offer their support to their sick friend, their visits left them with the feeling that it was Chiara who was supporting them. In her company, they experienced the love of God himself.

Blessed Chiara Badano made loving God and others the mission of her life. By God's grace, she was able to love unselfishly even though she suffered terribly.

Prayer for Love

Dear God of Love,
I love you and offer you my love as the only true gift I can give to you. Help me to love you more each day. Show me how to love and serve others, out of love for you. Teach me to recognize you in everyone I meet, and to treat others with kindness. Keep me from thinking only of myself, even when things are hard for me. Make every moment of my life a mission of your love. Amen.

How Can I Be a Hero of Love?

Is there a disappointment or frustration that I could offer to God with love? Is there a joy or accomplishment I can give him?

What can I do to treat others as I would like to be treated?

Other people have needs and wants just like I do. What can I do to remember that I am called to think of others even when I have struggles of my own?

Have I been able to express the love I have for God and other people? If so, how? If not, how might I communicate love better in the future?

What is the mission of my life? What can I do every day to accomplish it?

Part III

The "Little" Virtues

Think about the last time you went to see a movie in the theatre. When the movie was over, did you stay and watch all the credits? If so, you saw a long list of names. First came the stars of the film, the famous actors and actresses in their leading roles. Then came more names, mostly ones you hadn't seen before. These are the people who designed and built the set, made the costumes, applied makeup to the stars, edited the film, and composed the music for the soundtrack. As you watched the movie, you were probably not thinking about these people or saying to yourself, "Wow! The wardrobe director did an excellent job selecting that dress!" But without all these behind-the-scenes workers, the movie couldn't have been made.

They are the "little stars" of the show, who make it possible for the "big stars" to do their job.

Saint Francis de Sales called some virtues the "little" virtues. The *little virtues*: humility, obedience, patience, and gentleness aren't dramatic or extraordinary. They don't make a big splash or draw a lot of attention. But they are the virtues we need every day. We practice the little virtues in ordinary ways in ordinary circumstances.

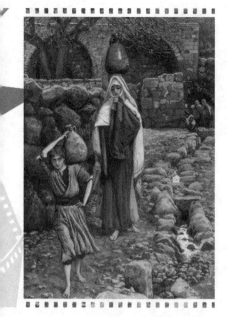

Many people dream of being recognized for some heroic display of virtue, in the way that we honor prisoners of war or a firefighter that saved a baby from a burning building. Most of us are rarely, if ever, afforded the opportunity for these stunning feats of virtue, just as most people who work on a movie aren't the starring actors. However, we *do* have the chance to do many little, ordinary things with excellence. We can practice the little virtues every day, no matter who we are and regardless of the circumstances of our life. The little virtues are ways of being great in small moments. It is possible to practice them in big—and even heroic—ways.

Jesus was the most virtuous person ever to have lived. He demonstrated every one of the great virtues to perfection. Yet when he described himself, Jesus did not speak of courage or justice. Instead, he emphasized the little virtues and chose to tell his followers that he was "gentle and humble of heart" (see Matthew 11:29).

Chapter 8

Humility and Saint Joan of Arc

What Is Humility?

Have you ever complimented someone's skill at something, only to have that person brush you off? If you compliment your friend on her excellent piano solo after a school concert and she says, "Oh no, I'm really terrible. I wasn't very good at all," you are left not knowing what to say in response. It feels awkward when this happens, because denying our achievements or expecting perfection from ourselves or others isn't true humility. On the other hand, it is much more truthful and humble if your friend responds by saying, "Thank you. I practiced a lot, and I am thankful to able to take lessons."

Humility is seeing ourselves the way God sees us.

> . . . Christ Jesus,
> who, though he was
> in the form of God. . .
> emptied himself,
> taking the form of a slave,
> being born in human likeness. . . .
> [H]e humbled himself
> and became obedient
> to the point of death—
> even death on a cross.
>
> Philippians 2:5–8

When we are humble, we have a real understanding of who we are and who God created us to be, with all of our unique gifts and struggles, strengths and weaknesses. Humility isn't low self-esteem, and it doesn't mean that we have to hide our talents or pretend we don't have certain gifts. Truly humble people acknowledge where their talents come from, the role others have played in developing them, and that they are meant to also benefit others.

When Jesus healed a sick man on the Sabbath, many religious leaders criticized him and accused him of violating God's law. Although it infuriated many people, Jesus was not afraid to tell the truth about being the Son of God, and about his unique relationship to God the Father. He humbly said, "the Son can do nothing on his own, but only what he sees the Father doing; for whatever the Father does, the Son does likewise" (John 5:19). At its core, humility is about understanding reality: knowing who God is, who we are, and our place in creation.

Humility is the virtue that leads us to prayer, because if we are humble we recognize our need for God in every moment of our lives. Humble people also know their own smallness and weaknesses. Have you ever felt overwhelmed by a responsibility? Perhaps you were chosen to be the captain of your team or asked to help younger students prepare for their first Communion. While you were honored to be selected, you also may have felt intimidated by the responsibilities involved, or maybe not quite up to the task. You may have worried about whether you had the athletic and leadership skills to be a good captain, or what you would do if a second grader misbehaved or asked a question you couldn't answer. Being humble in these circumstances means doing your best with the gifts God has given you, asking for help when you need it, and trusting that God will give you everything you need.

Humility is often called the foundation of virtue because it is necessary in order to attain the other virtues. If we lack self-knowledge, we cannot make progress growing in holiness. If we are humble, however, we live in the truth and allow God to help us become all he created us to be.

Who Is Saint Joan of Arc?

Northern France, during the early 1400s

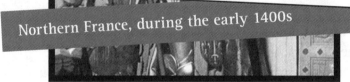

It was the fifteenth century, and France was at war with England. Joan and her family had been forced to flee their home and move to a new village. Joan was about thirteen years old when she knelt in her family's garden in a small French village. As she picked vegetables for that evening's supper, a bright light shone to her right and nearly blinded her. Joan turned toward it, in the direction of the town's parish church. From the light she heard a voice.

Confusion, awe, and fear filled Joan's heart. Was this a vision from God? Was it an angel? Why would an angel speak to her, a poor peasant girl kneeling in her family's garden in the middle of the afternoon? But over the

next several years, Joan continued to hear voices from heaven. She began to recognize the individual voices as the Archangel Michael, Saint Margaret, and Saint Catherine. In the beginning, the voices mostly encouraged her to be good and go to church. Eventually, however, the voices told Joan that God had chosen her to head the French army and lead them to victory over the English in the war.

"This is outrageous. A woman cannot fight in the army, much less command it," Joan protested. "I am sixteen and a girl! I cannot ride a horse, and I have no idea how to use a weapon."

"Go to Captain de Baudricourt. Tell him you will lead his men," came the reply. "God commands it."

Reluctantly, Joan asked a relative to take her to Vaucouleurs, a nearby town, where she approached Captain de Baudricourt. She knew she must have seemed insane to him, claiming that voices from heaven were telling her to command the French army. What mattered to Joan, however, was not what others thought of her, but being faithful to what God had called her to do. As she had anticipated, the captain laughed uproariously when he heard her request.

"You? A girl? Command my army? Go home, child. Your father should give you a good spanking!"

Joan did go home, but she returned some months later with the same request. In her humility, she knew that despite her inexperience and weakness, God would give her the skill and wisdom she needed to fulfill his call. Joan could offer no persuasive speech about her skills as a military commander—she had none. She could only express her confidence that following God's will would be best for the country of France. "Captain de Baudricourt, the French army has suffered an enormous loss at Orleans today. Please, let me lead. God commands it."

The captain stared at Joan in shock. How could she have known about the defeat at Orleans? There was no Internet in those days, no television, or radio. News spread slowly, if at all, to the peasant class. And yet, here stood Joan, telling him exactly what had happened in battle at Orleans earlier that day.

"How do you know this?" he demanded.

"A message from heaven," Joan replied.

Captain de Baudricourt sighed. On the one hand, what this girl was suggesting seemed outrageous and crazy. Voices and messages from heaven? Letting an unexperienced, young woman lead his men into battle against experienced soldiers? On the other hand, there was no other explanation for what she knew. He hesitated, but the English were crushing the French army. If there was a chance that what Joan was saying was true, he had to try. He placed her in command.

Joan could hardly believe that the captain had granted her request, especially since women were not permitted to serve in the army. She was quickly outfitted for battle. Joan wore pants, which only men did in those days. She rode into battle under a flag bearing the names of Jesus and Mary, declaring, "I am not afraid, for God is with me. I was born for this." Miraculously, the humble teenage girl led the French to a rousing defeat of the English forces, turning them back from Orleans.

The people of France loved Joan and believed that she would save them from the English. Joan, despite her popularity, never believed that she was more important than anyone else. In a situation that made her widely admired and highly esteemed, Joan may have been tempted to pride, but instead she remained humble. She knew that she was a simple farm girl, but she also knew that the Lord had chosen her to do something great.

Not surprisingly, the English were infuriated to have been defeated by a teenage girl and began to plot revenge. The following spring, Joan was captured by her enemies when an archer pulled her from her horse, and then sold her to the English as a prisoner. Once imprisoned, Joan was taken to trial. The English could not have her killed for beating them in battle, so they tried her as a heretic, or someone who spreads errors in faith.

Joan's interrogators demanded to know if she was in a state of grace and asked why an angel would choose a poor young girl such as herself, rather than a person of greater importance. Joan answered them, assuring the judges that she did not know why God had chosen her; she only knew that she was to follow his will and rely upon his grace. Alone, she could accomplish nothing, but God had given her all she needed for the tasks he laid before her.

For Joan, success was in humbly following God's will, nothing else. She was not concerned with what others thought of her. Though she certainly had no desire to leave her family and command armies, a task for which she had no skill or experience, she did it because God called her. Even when she was mocked and ridiculed, called crazy and a heretic, Joan did not back down from her vocation. Joan humbly followed Jesus where he led her, and she never turned back.

Saint Joan of Arc was humble when she accepted God's call, and she remained so even when she became famous and popular. Regardless of the cruel things others said about her, Saint Joan trusted in God to make up for what she lacked.

● ●
Prayer for Humility

Dear God of Greatness and Truth,
grant me the gift of true humility. May I always know that you have created me in love and have given me gifts, talents, and a purpose. Help me not to be afraid of being myself. Help me not to seek praise and recognition, attention or fame for their own sake. Instead, help me do what you have called me to do and use the gifts you have given me for your glory and not mine. Amen.

How Can I Train to Be a Hero of Humility?

What are the gifts and talents God has given me? What can I do to express thanks to God and use them well?

If I wanted to brag about something, what would it be? How might I choose to compliment someone else instead?

Am I afraid to share my gifts? How and when can I do what God asks of me, even if it makes others think I am weird or different?

Have I ever felt bad about myself or thought that I was unimportant? What can I do if I notice that someone else is feeling that way?

Which gifts do I wish God had given me? How can I use my special gifts to bring honor and glory to God?

Chapter 9

Obedience and Blessed Dina Bélanger

What Is Obedience?

Obedience is respecting authority, keeping the rules, and doing the right thing even when it means sacrificing our own will or desires. We aren't obedient simply for the sake of doing what other people say. When we choose to obey the people that God has put in authority over us, we practice bringing our will into line with God's will. People who have authority over us include our parents, teachers, coaches, pastors, bishops, and the pope.

When Jesus was twelve, he traveled with his parents to Jerusalem to observe the Passover. Though his parents were unaware of it, Jesus stayed behind when the rest of their group left to return home to Nazareth. Mary and Joseph frantically returned to Jerusalem to search for Jesus

> For just
> as by the one
> man's disobedience
> the many were made
> sinners, so by the one
> man's obedience the many
> will be made righteous.
>
> Romans 5:19

when they realized he was not with them. They found him in the Temple, listening to the teachers and asking questions. Although he was the Son of God, he came home to Nazareth with Mary and Joseph "and was obedient to them" (Luke 2:51). Jesus showed his obedience to the will of God by obeying the earthly parents God had given him.

When a coach gives in-structions at soccer practice, an obedient player follows his instructions. When a parent makes a rule about what time to be home for dinner, an obedient child comes home on time. But what if some-one in a position of authority gives us instructions to do something that is wrong or dangerous? The virtue of obedience does not include doing anything that is immoral or wrong. We never have to

obey a person who commands us to break God's laws. God would never ask us to do something that is wrong, and he has ultimate authority over everyone. Because God is our good Creator, our obedience to him can and should be unlimited. Faithful obedience keeps the commandments given by God. God's commands are always good for us. They keep us safe and happy, and they are an invitation to share in God's divine life.

Like a good army captain who wants to lead and protect his soldiers when he gives commands, God wills what is best for us and has a broader perspective than our own. Obedience to God is different from a soldier's obedience to his commander, however, because it is part of an ongoing conversation and relationship. Knowing and obeying God's will requires us to be in prayerful dialogue with him. In prayer, we can listen to God speaking to our hearts and discern his call in our life. When we "hear" God speak to us, we can ask questions or tell him our objections, and wait for his answers. Unlike a military commander, God welcomes our questions, fears, and hesitations, and he wants to answer them in order to help us freely say "yes" to him.

Who Is Blessed Dina Bélanger?

Quebec, Canada, around the year 1900

Sitting in daily Mass in her hometown of Quebec City, Canada, Dina looked out of the corners of her eyes at her mother in the pew. Sure she was not being watched, Dina reached into the pocket of her dress and pulled out Valeda, her doll. As she was marching Valeda down the back of the pew in front of her, Dina accidentally marched her right in front of Mama. Mama stared at Dina and whispered, "Put Valeda *away*!" Dina complied, but a few minutes later, she pulled Valeda back out. Mama took the doll from Dina and tucked it into her handbag.

At home, Mama hid Valeda, but she underestimated how determined Dina was to get her doll back. Dina searched the house from top to bottom until she found Valeda. At Mass the next morning, out came Valeda. Mama was furious.

"We will have to give Valeda to another little girl," Mama told Dina at supper that evening, "since she is causing such trouble in our family."

"No!" shrieked four-year-old Dina. "She is mine! You can't give her away!" Dina sprang out of her chair and began to stomp her feet and sob with rage. Papa rose from his own chair and began to imitate Dina's temper tantrum. Dina froze, her mouth hanging open at the spectacle before her. Realizing how ridiculous she looked, Dina stopped her tantrum and sat down, silent and embarrassed. Dina was still very young, but this experience helped her to see that her parents valued obedience and would not accept disrespect.

Years later, when she wrote her autobiography, Dina expressed her deep gratitude for the gift of parents who truly loved her enough to correct her faults and save her from her own weaknesses. Dina thanked God for parents who taught her the value of obedience. Her parents also impressed the importance of generosity, charity, and self-discipline on Dina. Dina accompanied her mother on visits to the poor and sick and was encouraged to share her belongings with others. When Dina was eight years old, her parents began taking her for regular piano lessons. They stressed the importance of practice and commitment to this new skill. Dina quickly progressed and demonstrated great musical talent.

At that time, children were generally not permitted to

receive their first Holy Communion until after their tenth birthday. Dina longed to receive Jesus in the Eucharist.

When she was just nine years old, Dina begged, "Please Mama, will you ask the priest if I can receive Jesus *now*?" Her mother informed Dina that she would not ask for her, but she would take Dina to the rectory to ask Father herself.

"I'm sorry," answered Father, "but I cannot allow it. I need to follow the guidelines of the Church."

Dina felt her heart drop and her eyes well up with tears of disappointment, but she swallowed hard and managed to say obediently, "Thank you for seeing us this morning, Father. I will wait until my next birthday and do my best to prepare until then."

Alhough she wasn't permitted to receive her first Holy Communion when she wanted to, Dina realized that the extra time was actually a gift. It gave her the opportunity for better preparation to receive all the graces offered to her in Communion.

At sixteen, Dina approached her parents with another special request. This time she wanted permission to enter a convent and become a religious sister. Dina's parents told her to ask her pastor and her spiritual director to see what they would say. Much as she had done as a child who wanted to receive Holy Communion early, Dina did not hesitate to ask others if they thought she was ready.

"I think that you are too young to make such a momentous decision," said her spiritual director, Monsignor Cloutier. "I don't doubt your vocation, but I believe it would be best to delay the decision until you are older and have more life experience." Dina's pastor agreed with her spiritual director.

Tears of disappointment flowed down Dina's cheeks. She had been so certain that this was what Jesus was asking of her. And yet, she had been advised by the two priests she trusted most to wait before entering. Dina resolved to accept this direction and wait until the appropriate time to enter the convent. Although the disappointment and ache did not leave, her heart was flooded with peace at knowing that she was being obedient to God's will. Later Dina would realize that this was a wise decision, as the delay of her entrance allowed her to see that the order of nuns she had originally sought to join was not the place to which Jesus was calling her. This obedience in accepting a delay of her plans would later allow Dina to discover her true spiritual home in the Congregation of Jesus and Mary.

While Dina waited to devote her life to Christ alone, she did not mope around. She used her time of waiting well. Dina studied, practiced the piano, and took part in normal social activities. Dina's heart belonged to God alone, but for now he was calling her to wait and live like other

young girls until the time she would be ready to fulfill her heart's desire and enter religious life.

Since Dina was a gifted musician, as a graduation present her parents offered her the opportunity to leave her home in Quebec to study music for two years in New York City. Dina's father escorted her and two other young girls on their long journey from Canada to New York in 1916. Dina was excited by the move and opportunity to study piano more seriously, but she did worry that she would be homesick living so far from her parents.

Upon arriving at the boarding house where they were staying, the girls discovered that there were two rooms left, a single and a double. Dina silently wished for her own room. She relished her solitude and found it tiring to make conversation. But Dina's father suggested, "Dina, why don't you and Bernadette share the double room, and Aline can have the single?" Dina was disappointed, but she agreed. She didn't want to hurt Bernadette's feelings and it was a chance to offer a small sacrifice to Jesus. To Dina's surprise, she and Bernadette grew to become as close as sisters and enjoyed their time together. Dina's sacrifice of obedience had turned out to be a great gift; she gained a dear friend and had learned that obedience can lead to joy.

Dina found many opportunities to exercise obedience in ordinary life. She was able to recognize God's will for her, shown in the directions given by her parents, pastor, and spiritual director. Every time, Dina chose God's will over her own. Each of these small decisions led Dina to the gift of her vocation and brought her great joy.

Dina's motto perhaps best sums up her obedience: "Love, and let Jesus and Mary have their way."

Blessed Dina Bélanger was obedient to her parents, her pastor, and her spiritual director, and she wait-ed for the things she wanted. Because she learned how to obey, Dina's life was filled with peace and many unexpected blessings along the way.

Prayer for Obedience

Dear God, Heavenly Father and King, help me to recognize your will and find joy in doing it. Remind me that it is also your will that I obey my parents, pastor, and others in authority over me, as long as they don't ask me to do something that is against your commandments. Give me the grace to remember that when I am asked to make a sacrifice of obedience, it is always for my good and ultimate happiness. Help me learn to trust your will more than my own. Amen.

How Can I Train to Be a Hero of Obedience?

When do I find it hard to obey people in authority over me? What can I do in those moments, especially when others are not being obedient?

How can I more closely follow the instructions of my parents, teachers, pastor, and others who are responsible for me?

Knowing that it will lead me to joy, how can I ask God to show me his will and to give me the grace to follow it?

What are examples of small sacrifices I could offer to God out of obedience to him?

Instead of insisting on having my own way, how can I practice listening to the opinions and directions of those around me?

Chapter 10

123

Patience and Saint Monica

What Is Patience?

When we are patient, we can wait for good things, endure suffering, and face disappointment. Patience gives us the ability to accept not getting our way. We don't complain, become angry, or feel sorry for ourselves when things don't happen the way we think they should. The virtue of patience has three stages. The "beginner level" of patience involves waiting without complaining. If we reach the "intermediate level" of patience, we do more than just "wait it out"; we accept hardships and allow them to help us grow in holiness. Finally, those who are "experts" at patience are actually grateful when they have to wait because they know that waiting is a powerful way to grow in virtue and love for God.

> May you be made strong with all the
> strength that comes from his glorious
> power, and may you be prepared to
> endure everything with patience,
> while joyfully giving thanks to the
> Father . . .   Colossians 1:11–12

Jesus is the supreme expert at patience. During the years of his public ministry, Jesus spent most of his time with his Apostles. But the Apostles frequently misunderstood what he was trying to teach them.

On one occasion, the Apostles James and John told Jesus that they wanted him to give them whatever they asked. Jesus didn't rebuke them or ask them who they thought they were. He simply asked what they wanted of him. When James and John answered that they wanted to sit at his side in glory, he patiently explained that they didn't understand what they were asking for, and like him, they would be called "not to be served but to serve" (Mark 10:45). It would have been easy to yell at James and John for completely missing the point about everything Jesus was trying to teach them. But Jesus never lost his temper with disciples who failed to understand his message; he patiently taught the lesson again in a different way to help them learn.

Patience is a virtue that we are given the opportunity to practice nearly every day. Have you ever had a younger child follow you around and ask you to explain everything and include them in your activities? Patience! Has an adult ever told you to wait or hold on when you ask for something? Patience! Life is full of little annoyances that can help us practice patience.

We can also practice patience when something unfair and hurtful happens.

When something is unfair, sometimes God asks us to patiently await the rest of his plan. Have you ever tried out for a play or sports team and not made the cut, despite having worked really hard? Patience! Patience is closely related to our trust in God. The more we trust God, the more we know that his plan is best for us. That kind of trust enables us to wait for his plan.

If we practice patience enough, we may even learn how to happily accept things that are difficult. That becomes possible when we know that God can and often does turn the worst circumstances into something good for us. Unfair things can happen in our lives, and sometimes it is impossible to change them. Patience helps us to endure and accept these situations trusting that God can help us become holier through difficulty.

Who Is Saint Monica?

North Africa (present-day Tunisia), during the mid-300s

Monica stood on the dock in the port of Carthage, a North African city. Her eyes scanned the crowd, trying to pick out her son, but in her heart she knew Augustine was not there. Monica had wanted to accompany him to Rome, but Augustine had no intention of allowing that to happen. He was twenty-eight years old, successful, and attractive, and he intended to enjoy himself in Rome without his devoutly Christian mother following on his heels. Augustine had told Monica that he was going to say good-bye to a friend before setting sail. But while she passed the evening praying in the nearby chapel of Saint Cyprian, he slipped away and boarded a ship without saying good-bye to her.

Monica's eyes filled with tears as she realized what had happened. *Augustine*, she pleaded silently, *why do you do this?* For many years Monica had prayed for her son's con-

version to the Catholic faith. She often spoke with him about the sinful choices he was making and his false beliefs. He had rejected Christianity as childish and unworthy of his intellect. Monica suffered greatly out of concern for Augustine's soul. What would become of this young man who loved parties and pleasures, but cared nothing about truth? Monica stood weeping on the dock, hurt by her son's deceit and grieving for his lost and wandering soul. Monica prayed fervently for her son as she walked through the city toward her home.

But Monica would not give up. This was merely the latest setback in her nearly three-decades-long quest to bring her son home to the Catholic Church. When Augustine was a small boy, Monica had unsuccessfully begged her non-Christian husband, Patricius, to allow her to raise their children as Catholics. When Augustine fell gravely ill as a teenager, Monica at last prevailed upon Patricius to allow his Baptism, but when Augustine's health began to improve, Patricius revoked his consent, insisting that it was no longer necessary. When Augustine became a wild, carousing young man, Monica entreated a bishop to speak with him. He refused on the grounds that Augustine was too stubborn and not yet ready to accept the truth.

"God will reach him," the bishop had told her. Monica persevered, weeping in desperation for her son's soul. "It is not possible that the son you have cried so many tears for should be lost," he assured her.

Determined to bring her son to Christ, Monica followed him over the sea to Rome. The ocean was rough and the journey perilous. The ship was tossed about as cold water rocked its sides and the wind roared around the travelers. Even the sailors were frightened by the elements they faced. In an unusual reversal of roles, Monica comforted the crew, assuring them that she knew they would arrive safely, as God had granted her a vision of her reunion with the son whom she was sailing to see. Monica was right; she and the ship's crew, as well as the other passengers, arrived safely. But by the time she arrived, Augustine had moved on to a new job in the city of Milan. Monica was not dissuaded.

When at last Monica found Augustine in Milan, she was rewarded with the happy news that Augustine had met Ambrose, the bishop of Milan. Monica thanked God for having answered her many prayers. Here, at last, was an equally brilliant mind who could shepherd Augustine along the path in his journey toward God.

Monica set up a home in Milan and lived there, patiently waiting and praying for Augustine to find the truth. She also befriended Bishop Ambrose and spent her days in church, listening intently to his homilies and visiting the chapels of various saints to intercede for her son. Slowly, bit by bit, Augustine was becoming convinced that the Catholic faith was true.

In August of 386, Augustine announced what his mother had waited all her life to hear. He had accepted the teachings of the Catholic faith in full, and he had asked to be baptized. On Easter in 387, Augustine was at last baptized in Milan by Ambrose. Monica's tears of petition and anguish turned to tears of joy.

Shortly after Augustine's Baptism, Monica and he decided to return to North Africa. One afternoon they stood in an upstairs window of their temporary home in the town of Ostia, where they were preparing to set sail. The land journey from Milan to Ostia had been tiring, and they still faced the uncertainty of the sea voyage back to Carthage, but both mother  and son were filled with peace. The sound of their friends laughing could be heard in the distance, and the two stood in the sunshine gazing into the lush garden below.

Finally united in Christ, Monica and Augustine discussed what heaven would be like when at last they reached their eternal home. As they spoke, God granted them the gift of a mystical experience, beyond words or senses. This grace allowed them to truly understand the words of Jesus when he spoke of the good and faithful servant being invited to "enter into the joy of [the] Master" (Matthew 25:23). Neither Augustine nor Monica could fully describe what they experienced that day, but on that sun-drenched afternoon in Ostia, mother and son were briefly granted a moment in which they knew the joy that would be theirs forever in heaven.

All Monica's earthly hopes were accomplished. She had seen her son abandon his sinful ways and had shared in the joy of his conversion. The waiting, which had seemed endless, was over. Augustine's wanderings had concluded in his arrival at his true spiritual home: the Church. Monica's patient prayers, sacrifices, and actions at last bore the fruit that she had long hoped for. She told her son that God had granted her more than she had imagined. Her soul was now flooded with the peace and contentment that God gave to her for her long years of perseverance and patience, doing what she could while waiting and trusting him to bring about Augustine's conversion.

Saint Monica was patient for many years as she waited for her son Augustine to find salvation in Jesus Christ. She never ceased to pray and offer sacrifices to God for his conversion.

Prayer for Patience

Dear God of Time and Eternity,
help me to be patient and to wait for you to show me your will. Help me to bear annoyances and even wrongs gracefully, to draw closer to you when I suffer, and to look for your presence in every circumstance. Give me the virtue of patience, so that your grace shines through me when I deal with others. Show me your presence in every step of my journey, and give me confidence in the plan you have for me. Amen.

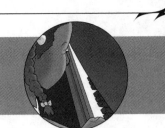

How Can I Train to Be a Hero of Patience?

How can I remember to take the time to help my younger siblings or elderly relatives and include them in my activities?

When I really want something, like a treat, or am impatient for something, like a special occasion, what can I do to wait with patience and without complaining?

When has someone been patient with me? How did that make me feel?

What is an example of a time that I can ask, "How can I help?" instead of asking, "When can I . . . ?"

When have I felt the most impatient? How can I practice patience in this circumstance?

Chapter 11

Gentleness and Saint Charbel Makhlouf

What Is Gentleness?

Gentleness, or "meek-ness" as it is often called in Scripture, can be mistaken for weakness. In fact, nothing is stronger than gentleness. It takes a lot of self-control to be gentle!

Jesus told us how we could become more like him when he said, ". . . learn from me, for I am gentle and humble in heart" (Matthew 11:29). When Jesus called people to repentance, he also did so gently. The Pharisees brought a woman who had been caught in sin before Jesus, demanding to know what he thought should be done, since the law said she should be stoned. Instead of trying to show his strength by condemning the woman, Jesus challenged the crowd

"Take my yoke upon you and learn from me; for I am gentle and humble in heart, and you will find rest for your souls." Matthew 11:29

to look carefully at the truth of their own lives. "Let anyone among you who is without sin be the first to throw a stone at her," Jesus said (John 8:7). One by one, the people dropped their stones and walked away. After the Pharisees left, Jesus spoke gently to the woman, assuring her that he did not condemn her but also instructing her not to sin again. Jesus' gentle approach invited people to draw closer to him in conversion.

Have you ever heard someone say, "Be gentle!" to someone who is holding a baby or small animal? Perhaps when you were very young, your parents told you to "use gentle hands" when turning the pages of a book or holding a fragile item. We are often urged to be gentle in caring for people or things that are weaker than we are. Our strength can easily hurt a tiny baby or damage a glass vase, so we take care to be gentle in order to protect them from harm. But we can and should approach everything with gentleness in order to protect what is valuable and precious.

Gentleness applies to taking care of someone's physical well-being, but it also applies to the way we care for another person's mind and soul. If we are gentle, we are careful not to hurt others by the way we behave or treat them.

You may have seen professional athletes ejected from games or fined for an uncontrolled temper or angry outbursts. Gentleness is a virtue that would help these athletes exercise self-control, stay in the game, and avoid penalties. The virtue of gentleness trains us to control how we express our emotions so that they may be used for the good of others, and not to hurt or bully them. This does not mean that a gentle person is never angry, or that negative emotions are wrong. A gentle person, however, expresses anger and other feelings in a calm and constructive way that does not hurt others.

Virtue makes us powerful in a holy way and fills us with God's strength. Through gentleness, we fully respect and care for the dignity God has given to every person.

Who Is Saint Charbel Makhlouf?

Lebanon, during the mid-1800s

Youssef scrambled over the rocky hillside, leading his family's cow to pasture. When they arrived at a grassy spot, Youssef slipped the rope from around the cow's neck so that she could graze comfortably.

Once she had eaten enough, Youssef told her, "Rest now, Zahra. I want to pray. And wait until I finish my prayers please, because I cannot talk to you and God at the same time."

Youssef climbed a little higher up the steep slope, toward his special spot. As he made his way up, he picked wild flowers, tucking them under his arm. Then, when he had nearly reached his destination, Youssef ran into

a group of boys from his small Lebanese village of Bekaa Kafra.

"Hey look, it's The Saint! He's passing by. We better get his blessing!" called the boys. The boys in Youssef's village often called him "The Saint," because he spent so much time praying and was a faithful altar server at Mass.

Youssef smiled uncertainly at the boys as he approached. Although they teased him, they also played together in their small close-knit village. Youssef was hurt by their taunts, but they were the boys he had grown up with and he wanted to get along with them.

"What's up, Youssef? Where are you going?" asked one of the boys.

"To the grotto," he answered with a shy smile.

"Not again! Listen, we have an idea. There's no need for you to go today. The chickpeas Abu planted are ready to be harvested. Come with us. We'll just take a few."

"No thanks, I'm on my way to the grotto," repeated Youssef as he stepped past the other boys and continued on his way. Stealing from the parish priest's garden wasn't something Youssef would ever have done.

"Go, go! I want to see what you'll get from this grotto in the end. Maybe you've planted some chickpeas in there that we don't know about!" teased the boys.

Youssef could still hear the laughter of the boys behind him as he slipped into a crevice in the rocky hillside and crawled into the small grotto. He knelt before the cross he had made of two branches lashed together, and the prayer card of the Blessed Mother and baby Jesus, which hung above the cross. Carefully, he laid the bouquet he'd gathered in front of the cross and began to sing a song that he had learned at his parish church.

"Your Son is wounded and suffering,
and he has suffered for me.
Give me a share of him. O Holy Mother,
print the wounds of your only child in my heart."

As Youssef knelt in prayer, he heard a commotion at the entrance of the grotto. It sounded like the boys who had been teasing him.

"He's still following us!" gasped one of the boys. He sounded winded and frightened. Youssef paused his prayer.

"What is it? What's wrong?" he called out to the boys at the grotto's entrance.

"It's Abu! He saw us in the chickpea field. He sent his dog after us. We only took a few! That priest is so stingy, and that dog is crazy." The distant sound of barking grew closer as the dog approached the grotto.

"Well, you better come inside the grotto then," said Youssef. The boys scrambled in, frantic to escape the dog pursuing them. Youssef climbed outside the grotto and looked around. The dog came loping around a rock and slowed when she saw Youssef. Youssef crouched down and held out his hand toward the dog.

"Here, girl. It's okay. Come here." Youssef held out a piece of bread. The shaggy dog whined quietly and then inched forward, taking the bread from Youssef's hand. Then the dog lay down to eat while Youssef scratched her back. Behind Youssef, the other boys stood in a group at the mouth of the grotto, stunned that the barking, snapping dog that had chased them from the chickpea field seemed to have transformed at Youssef's hands.

Youssef did not beat the dog back or taunt the boys who had come running to him for help after mocking him. Instead, he let his gentleness prove his strength. Young Youssef was an example of gentleness in the way he treated all those around him. When the boys laughed at him for praying in his grotto and then later came running to him for a place to hide, it would have been easy for Youssef to turn them away and leave them to what they deserved. Instead, Youssef acted with a gentle and merciful heart, welcoming the frightened boys into the grotto. He then went out to confront the dog that was chasing them. Even the mad dog was tamed by Youssef's gentle spirit!

Youssef continued to shepherd his family's animals for the rest of his childhood and teenage years. In 1851, when he was twenty-three years old, Youssef left home to join a monastery, where he eventually became a priest. His religious name was Father Charbel. He continued to spend much of his time in prayer. His desire was to love with a heart like the gentle Heart of Jesus. As he grew older, Father Charbel became known and loved for his gentleness toward all. Father Charbel died on Christmas Eve 1898, as the snow fell and the world prepared to celebrate the birth of our gentle God who came to us as a helpless baby. After Father Charbel's burial, a bright light was seen coming from his grave. Many miraculous healings have been attributed to his intercession. In death, Saint Charbel has followed in the footsteps of Jesus, the Gentle Healer.

*Saint Charbel Makhlouf
was gentle with everyone
he encountered.
He continually showed
care and concern for
others, especially
those who were
weaker than he.*

Prayer for Gentleness

Dear God of Gentleness and Strength,
give me a heart as gentle as the Heart of Jesus.
Teach me how to show care and kindness, especially toward those who are weaker than I am. Give me the strength to express my feelings in a way that does not hurt others. Help me always to protect the people and things in my care. Amen.

How Can I Train to Be a Hero of Gentleness?

What are some ways I can help or protect those who may be weaker than I am?

How can I act gently in caring for younger siblings, younger students at school, my pets, and my belongings?

When I feel angry, what are some ways I might express how I feel without hurting anyone or damaging anything?

How can I show kindness to the people around me, even when their actions or words make me feel angry or irritated?

How do I think of the people in my life who choose to be kind and gentle? Do I see them as weak or strong?

You Can Be a Hero

There are as many ways to be holy as there are people. The saints come from every country, every time period, every age, every walk of life, and every type of family. Though there is enormous diversity in their circumstances, every saint lives a virtuous life: a life powered by God himself. With the power of the virtues flowing through their lives, the superpowers of the saints are endless!

Just as God calls each person to a one-of-a-kind holiness, each time and place needs a different kind of hero. During Hitler's occupation of Poland, the world needed a hero like Saint John Paul II who knew how to resist the Nazis. When Christianity first came to Korea, the Church needed heroes who could be witnesses to Christ even when they faced torture by the Korean authorities. As

World War I engulfed Europe, the Church needed heroes who would teach us to pray and sacrifice for peace.

You were born at exactly the right time and place in history to be the person God created you to be. No matter the specific circumstances of your life, you are called to be holy too, right here and now and in everyday ways. You don't have to wait to be older or for your life to be different.

You have the opportunity to grow in holiness *today*. What kind of hero is needed in the situations of your life? Do you have friends who seem "lost" and need an example of faith in God? Is there some-one in your class who is lonely or bullied and needs someone to show them God's love? When you look at the world around you, do you see wrongs that need to be addressed by someone committed to justice? These types of situations are the way that God is showing you what kind of holy hero he is calling you to be.

Every time you train to practice the virtues, you are an example of God's goodness to the world around you. Now think of a time you've demonstrated one of the virtues in your own life. For example, you might remember that when your mom asked you to set the table for dinner last night, you obeyed the first time you were asked.

Some of the virtues may come quite easily to you. Maybe you love helping younger children and are naturally a patient person. Other virtues may be more of a struggle for you. Perhaps you are inclined to spend hours playing video games and struggle to be temperate. As Christians we can draw inspiration from the example of Jesus and the saints. The saints can encourage us to continue practicing those virtues we excel at, and grow in those virtues that are more difficult for us. Virtuous people are a gift to the world around them because they are using their powers for good; they are building the kingdom of God.

● ● ● ● ● ● ● ● ● ● ● ● ● ● ● ● ●
Prayer for Virtue

Dear God of Goodness,
make me strong with your strength;
make me virtuous! Send your Holy
Spirit to show me how I can be
holy in my own life, right here and
now, and give me the graces I need
to become more like Jesus every
day. Show me what kind of hero is
needed where I am, and help me to
be that hero. Help me to build your
kingdom here until the day you
bring me, and all those I love, to
heaven. Amen.

Litany for the Virtues of the Saints

Saint John Paul II, we ask your prayers for prudence.
Pray for us.

Blessed Pier Giorgio Frassati, we ask your prayers for justice.
Pray for us.

Saints Peter Yu Tae-chol and Agatha Yi, we ask your prayers
for fortitude. *Pray for us.*

Venerable Matt Talbot, we ask your prayers for temperance.
Pray for us.

Lucia dos Santos, Blesseds Jacinta and Francisco Marto, we
ask your prayers for faith. *Pray for us.*

Saint Josephine Bakhita, we ask your prayers for hope.
Pray for us.

Blessed Chiara Luce Badano, we ask your prayers for love.
Pray for us.

Saint Joan of Arc, we ask your prayers for humility.
Pray for us.

Blessed Dina Bélanger, we ask your prayers for obedience.
Pray for us.

Saint Monica, we ask your prayers for patience.
Pray for us.

Saint Charbel Makhlouf, we ask your prayers for gentleness.
Pray for us.

All holy men and women of God, pray that God will give us
the grace to follow your examples of virtue. Amen.

How Can I Train to Be a Hero of Virtue?

Which virtues come most easily to you, and how have you practiced them? Which virtues are most difficult for you? How can you grow in the virtues that challenge you most?

Which story of virtue was most inspiring to you? What lessons from that story can you put into practice in your own life?

What kind of saintly example of virtue would be most helpful to you right now?

What kind of virtuous people has God placed in your life? Which virtues do they excel at? What have you learned from their examples?

What kind of saint is God calling you to be? What virtues is God asking you to practice in order to be a holy hero for him?

Appendix

Brief Biographies

Pope Saint John Paul the Great

John Paul II was born Karol Wojtyla on May 18, 1920 in Wadowice, Poland. As a young man, Karol loved swimming, skiing, and performing in the theatre. Karol's university was closed as a result of the Nazi occupation, so he

 began studying at a secret seminary in Krakow and was ordained a priest in 1946. Father Wojtyla later became Archbishop Wojtyla of Krakow and participated in the Second Vatican Council. In 1978, he was elected pope and took the name John Paul II. He was the first non-Italian pope in 400 years! On the Feast of Our Lady of Fatima in 1981, Pope John Paul II was shot in Saint Peter's Square in an assassination attempt. He gave credit to the Blessed Mother for saving his life. He was known for his extensive travels all over the world, his prolific writing, and the numerous men and women he canonized as saints.

John Paul II died April 2, 2005 and was canonized April 27, 2014. His feast day is celebrated on October 22, and he is among the patron saints of World Youth Day, a tradition he began.

Blessed Pier Giorgio Frassati

Pier Giorgio Frassati was born in Turin, Italy, on April 6, 1901 to wealthy, socially active parents. Neither of his parents were particularly religious or active in the faith. His father was the founder and director of the newspaper *La Stampa* and an active politician; his mother was a painter. Pier Giorgio became deeply committed to his faith at an early age. He attended daily Mass, was active in sev-

eral Catholic youth organizations, and often spent his nights in Eucharistic Adoration. Pier Giorgio was especially concerned about social justice issues, had a deep love for the poor, and opposed the rise of Italian Fascist dictator Benito Mussolini. He excelled at sports and frequently led his friends in mountain climbing expeditions and ski trips. He died of polio on July 4, 1925. Thousands of the people he helped came to his funeral. In 1981 his remains were found incorrupt, that is, without decay, and his body was transferred to the cathedral in Turin.

Pier Giorgio was beatified on May 20, 1990 by Pope John Paul II who called him a "Man of the Beatitudes." His feast day is celebrated on July 4, and he is among the patron saints of World Youth Day.

Saints Peter Yu Tae-chol and Agatha Yi

Peter Yu Tae-chol and Agatha Yi are among the 103 Korean Martyrs. In nineteenth-century Korea, Christianity was condemned by the Korean government and Christians were persecuted and killed. John Paul II canonized the Korean martyrs on May 6, 1984.

Peter was born in 1826. His father, Augustine Nyou Tjin-kil, was a Christian and served as a government interpreter. Like Peter, he was also martyred for his faith. Peter's mother and sisters were not Christians. Peter turned himself in as a Christian when he was just thirteen years old. He died in prison on October 31, 1839.

Agatha was born in 1822. With her parents and brother, she was incarcerated in 1839 for her Christian faith. After being imprisoned for nine months, separated from her parents, threatened, and beaten, Agatha was strangled to death in Seoul on January 9, 1840.

Agatha's and Peter's feast day is celebrated on September 20, and they are among the patron saints of Korea.

Venerable Matt Talbot

Matt Talbot was born into a poor family in Dublin, Ireland, in 1856. He was the second of twelve children. When Matt was twelve years old, he had to leave school in order to help support his family. Matt began sampling the wine and liquor in the store where he worked and was an alcoholic by the time he was thirteen.

When he was twenty-eight, Matt decided to stop drinking and mend his life. He worked as a laborer in a lumberyard and was known for being an honest and hard worker. After getting sober, Matt began to visit churches all over Dublin and spent his free time praying and reading the Bible and lives of the saints. Matt remained sober until his death in 1925.

In 1965, Pope Paul VI recognized his sanctity and declared Matt "Venerable." His feast day is celebrated on June 19, and he is the patron saint of those struggling with alcoholism and addiction.

The Children of Fatima

Lucia dos Santos and her cousins, Blesseds Jacinta and Francisco Marto, lived in a small Portuguese village outside the town of Fatima. Lucia was born in 1907, Francisco in 1908, and Jacinta in 1910.

In 1917, the Blessed Mother appeared to the three children in a field as they tended their family's flock of sheep. For six months, she appeared on the thirteenth day of each month at noon to encourage the children to pray the Rosary, do penance, and make sacrifices for sinners. On the day of Mary's final apparition, the Miracle of the Sun took place when the sun appeared to dance in the sky. It was witnessed by 70,000 people.

Francisco and Jacinta died of the influenza epidemic just a few years after the apparitions. Both were beatified on May 13, 2000. Because the Church only beatifies people who have died, Lucia was not beatified along with her cousins. Lucia became a Carmelite nun and died in 2005, at the age of ninety-seven.

The feast day of Francisco and Jacinta is celebrated on February 20, and they are the patron saints of people who suffer ridicule for their faith. The Feast of Our Lady of Fatima is celebrated on May 13.

Saint Josephine Bakhita

Bakhita was not this saint's original name, but the one given to her by the slave traders who kidnapped her from a field near her home in Sudan. She was just nine years old when she was kidnapped in 1877, and the trauma of her kidnapping caused her to forget her original name.

Many of the families that Bakhita served as a slave were cruel and abusive. Eventually, she was given as a "gift" to an Italian family and became their daughter's nanny. Bakhita and the little girl in her charge went to stay with the Canossian sisters in Italy. There, Bakhita learned about God and his great love for her. In 1890, she was baptized Josephine Margaret Fortunata, and refused to return to Sudan. Six years later she took vows as a Canossian sister.

She died in 1947 and was canonized October 1, 2000. Her feast day is celebrated on February 8, and she is the patron saint of Sudan.

Blessed Chiara Badano

Chiara's parents prayed for a child for eleven years, and at last Chiara was born in 1971 in Sasello, Italy. When Chiara was just nine years old, her friend introduced her to the Focolare movement in the Church. Focolare promotes unity and brotherhood among all people. Chiara

met and became close to the founder of Focolare, a woman who shared the same first name, Chiara Lubich. The younger Chiara found that Focolare helped her truly discover the Gospel and inspired her to make it the purpose of her life.

Chiara was a strong athlete who excelled at tennis. She was also a hard working student, but struggled in academics. Although Chiara had many friends, she was often teased by her classmates for her deep love of Jesus. At seventeen years old, Chiara was diagnosed with a deadly form of bone cancer. As she was dying in the hospital, Chiara brought joy to all those around her and planned her funeral as if it were her wedding day, the day she would become the bride of Christ.

Chiara died of cancer when she was just eighteen. Pope Benedict XVI beatified her on September 25, 2010. Her feast day is celebrated on October 29.

Saint Joan of Arc

Joan was born in 1412 in the village of Domremy, France. She was the daughter of medieval tenant farmers. When she was thirteen, Joan began to receive divine messages from Saint Michael. They encouraged her to fight in order to save France from England and to install Charles of Valois as King of France.

In an act of stunning audacity, Joan requested an army to fight the English. Even more unbelievably, she was given command to lead them into battle! As a seventeen-year-old girl, she set off for Orleans where she led an assault on the English forces, winning a miraculous victory for France. Shortly afterward, however, Joan was taken captive and sold to the English who accused her of being a witch, a heretic, and lying about the voices of the saints who spoke to her.

She was burned at the stake on May 30, 1431 in Rouen, France. Joan was canonized in 1920. Her feast day is celebrated on May 30, and she is a patron saint of France and soldiers.

Blessed Dina Bélanger

Dina was born in 1897 to devout French-Canadian parents. She lived in Quebec and was a gifted pianist. As a teen, she spent two years studying piano at the New York Conservatory. Upon returning to Canada, she gave concerts for charitable causes.

Although she had a lively social life, Dina often longed to be alone with Jesus. In 1921, she entered the Congregation of Jesus and Mary as a religious sister. After entering the convent, she was given the task of giving music lessons to children. She contracted

scarlet fever from one of her students, and the disease soon developed into tuberculosis. While sick, Dina wrote her autobiography at the request of her superior. She died in September of 1929.

Pope John Paul II beatified Dina on March 20, 1993. Her feast day is celebrated on September 4, and she is the patron of those who do not have a saint's name.

Saint Monica

Monica was born in 331 in North Africa, in what is modern day Algeria. Her parents arranged her marriage to a non-Christian of higher social status. Monica lived with her husband, Patricius, and his mother, both of whom had bad tempers and were often cruel. Monica prayed for both of them for years and both eventually became Christians.

Monica and her husband had three children. Though he had a brilliant mind, their son Augustine was a constant source of worry for Monica. Monica prayed for him constantly, even chasing him down in Italy, and was rewarded when he finally converted to Christianity in 367. Monica died of a fever near Rome in the port city of Ostia when she was fifty-six-years-old. Monica's burial stone was lost for centuries, but rediscovered in 1945 by two boys digging a hole to plant a goal post! Although Monica did not live to witness it, Augustine went on to become a priest and then the bishop of Hippo, an important North African port. He also became well-known as a prolific writer and theologian and was canonized a saint.

Her feast day is August 27 (one day before her son's). Monica is the patron saint of wives, mothers, and abuse victims.

Saint Charbel Makhlouf

Youssef Makhlouf was born in 1828 in the village of Bekaa Kafra in the mountains of Lebanon. His father died when he was very young, but his mother remarried and Youssef was raised in a devout family with his siblings. Even as a child, Youssef was deeply religious. He was responsible for caring for the family's flock of animals, and often prayed in a small grotto while the animals grazed.

Youssef entered the monastery when he was twenty-three years old, and he took the name Charbel in honor of an early Christian martyr. In 1875, he received permission to live alone as a hermit caring for the small chapel of Saints Peter and Paul. Charbel died of a stroke in 1898.

He was canonized by Pope Paul VI in 1977 and is popular not only in Lebanon, but also in Mexico. His feast is celebrated on July 24, and he is the patron saint of Lebanon.

Julia Harrell is a lifelong lover of books and storytelling. She is a former elementary school teacher turned wife and stay-at-home mother. She holds a masters degree in Education from the University of Maryland and a masters in Theology from Franciscan University of Steubenville. She combines her two passions by writing children's literature about the Catholic faith. Julia is an avid runner, reader, and traveler who lives outside Washington, DC, with her husband and two young children.

![Pauline KIDS]

Who are the Daughters of St. Paul?

We are Catholic sisters with a mission. Our task is to bring the love of Jesus to everyone like Saint Paul did. You can find us in over 50 countries. Our founder, Blessed James Alberione, showed us how to reach out to the world through the media. That's why we publish books, make movies and apps, record music, broadcast on radio, perform concerts, help people at our bookstores, visit parishes, host JClub book fairs, use social media and the Internet, and pray for all of you.

Visit our Web site at www.pauline.org

BOOKS & MEDIA

The Daughters of St. Paul operate book and media centers at the following addresses. Visit, call, or write the one nearest you today, or find us at www.paulinestore.org.

CALIFORNIA
3908 Sepulveda Blvd, Culver City, CA 90230   310-397-8676
3250 Middlefield Road, Menlo Park, CA 94025   650-369-4230

FLORIDA
145 SW 107th Avenue, Miami, FL 33174   305-559-6715

HAWAII
1143 Bishop Street, Honolulu, HI 96813   808-521-2731

ILLINOIS
172 North Michigan Avenue, Chicago, IL 60601   312-346-4228

LOUISIANA
4403 Veterans Memorial Blvd, Metairie, LA 70006   504-887-7631

MASSACHUSETTS
885 Providence Hwy, Dedham, MA 02026   781-326-5385

MISSOURI
9804 Watson Road, St. Louis, MO 63126   314-965-3512

NEW YORK
64 West 38th Street, New York, NY 10018   212-754-1110

SOUTH CAROLINA
243 King Street, Charleston, SC 29401   843-577-0175

TEXAS — Currently no book center; for parish exhibits or outreach evangelization, contact: 210-569-0500 or SanAntonio@paulinemedia.com or P.O. Box 761416, San Antonio, TX 78245

VIRGINIA
1025 King Street, Alexandria, VA 22314   703-549-3806

CANADA
3022 Dufferin Street, Toronto, ON M6B 3T5   416-781-9131

• •

SMILE God loves you